ROY BENNETT

FORTISSIMO!

Teacher's Resource Book

CAMBRIDGE
UNIVERSITY PRESS

PUBLISHED BY THE PRESS SYNDICATE OF THE UNIVERSITY OF CAMBRIDGE
The Pitt Building, Trumpington Street, Cambridge, United Kingdom

CAMBRIDGE UNIVERSITY PRESS
The Edinburgh Building, Cambridge CB2 2RU, UK
40 West 20th Street, New York, NY 10011–4211, USA
10 Stamford Road, Oakleigh, VIC 3166, Australia
Ruiz de Alarcón 13, 28014 Madrid, Spain
Dock House, The Waterfront, Cape Town 8001, South Africa

http://www.cambridge.org

First published 1996
Third printing 2001

Printed in the United Kingdom at the University Press, Cambridge

A catalogue record for this book is available from the British Library

ISBN 0 521 56924 9

Cover illustration by Helen Manning

Components of the *fortissimo!* course
Students' Book ISBN 0 521 56923 0
Teacher's Resource Book ISBN 0 521 56924 9
Compact Discs (set of four) ISBN 0 521 56925 7

Acknowledgements
IT material is reproduced from the Notate music processing software package published by Longman Logotron.
Material from the National Curriculum is Crown Copyright and is reproduced by permission of the Controller of HMSO.

CONTENTS

Introduction

The course; the basic structure

Fortissimo! is a music course broadly aiming at Key Stage 4. It is structured in thirty chapters, each exploring one or more structural or expressive elements of music, concepts, or devices, which in many ways form the core of the music curriculum. Consideration has been given to the 'programmes of study' in music (reproduced below) as they relate to Key Stage 3, and to how these might usefully be built upon.

The components of the course

The components of *fortissimo!* consist of a students' book of 256 pages, this teacher's resource book, and a set of four compact discs.

The compact discs

The CDs contain 122 pieces and extracts of music from different periods (13th century to the 1990s), of various types and styles (classical, jazz, rock, folk, traditional), and from a variety of cultures and traditions, Western and non-Western.

The pieces and extracts have been chosen specifically to illustrate particular points and ideas, musical elements and concepts, composing styles and techniques. Regrettably, recordings of certain planned items of rock and 20th-century compositions have had to be omitted, due either to exorbitant cost or refusal to grant permission for inclusion.

While it is the intention that the course as a whole should treat all music equally, clear examples were the first criteria. In the case of certain compositional devices and techniques, the clearest – sometimes the only – examples are found in the repertoire of the Western 'classical' tradition, and consequently this has resulted in a higher proportion of such pieces.

Key Stage 3 Programme of Study

Pupils' understanding and enjoyment of music should be developed through activities that bring together requirements from both Performing and Composing and Listening and Appraising wherever possible.

1 **Pupils should be given opportunities to:**
- **a** use sounds and respond to music individually, in pairs, in groups and as a class;
- **b** make appropriate use of IT to explore, create and record sounds.

2 When performing, composing, listening and appraising, pupils should be taught to listen with understanding and identify the development of musical ideas, investigating, internalising and discriminating within and between the musical elements: pitch, duration, dynamics, tempo, timbre, texture and structure.

3 The repertoire chosen for performing and listening should extend pupils' musical experience and knowledge, and develop their appreciation of the richness of our diverse cultural heritage. It should include music in a variety of styles:
- **a** from the European 'classical' tradition, from its earliest roots to the present day;
- **b** from folk and popular music;
- **c** from the countries and regions of the British Isles;
- **d** from cultures across the world;
- **e** by well known composers and performers, past and present.

The students' book

The thirty chapters of the students' book are intended to be progressive, though teachers may prefer to select their own order. Some of the material will, of course, form a revision, or revisiting, of basic elements and concepts encountered in earlier years. It is hoped that work in such areas will reinforce and extend students' musical skills, knowledge and understanding.

While *fortissimo!* is aimed at 14–16 year olds taking GCSE, schools which have a strong programme for KS3 to 4 may wish to start using the book in Year 9. See page 16 for a map demonstrating how this might work.

It has been the intention, throughout the students' book, to provide as many Composing, Performing, and Listening opportunities as possible so that teachers may choose which to emphasize in each chapter according to their own schemes of work and the needs of individual students. It is therefore expected that the teacher will decide which activities and tasks are tackled by which students, according to their needs and abilities.

fortissimo! takes an integrated and holistic view of music in terms of teaching and learning. It is intended that most of the Composing tasks should be tackled by any ability, and occasionally some guidance is given. However, it is acknowledged that students may be operating at different levels in Performing, Composing and Listening. The three activities may not necessarily progress hand in hand, and therefore the Composing tasks in the students' book have mainly been worded to be as open-ended as possible.

A Composing activity often stems from a Listening activity – but teachers may sometimes prefer to reverse this order. There are opportunities for group, pair and individual work – in many instances, the decision being left open to the students or teacher (though it is probable that, at later stages, students will mostly be working individually).

It is expected that students will perform – or organize performances of – their completed and refined compositions. Some pieces, of course, will require group performance. In such cases, some suggested aims a student might consider when rehearsing and directing his/her own composition are given overleaf. It is intended that the following page should be photocopied and handed out to students.

Some suggested aims you might consider when rehearsing and directing your own composition

- Ensure (well in advance) appropriate, clear and accurate notation of the score/parts, with clear performance directions.
- Be thoroughly organized and prepared – knowing every detail of the music, and being absolutely clear about what you hope to achieve.
- Have confidence in, and enthusiasm for, your composition.
- Set up an easy, but firm and controlling, relationship with the performers.
- Communicate intentions, points and ideas about interpretation clearly to the performers – giving clear verbal instructions, and appropriate, clear visual signals, always maintaining adequate guidance and firm control.
- Recognize and identify errors of technique or interpretation, and work on them efficiently and productively.
- Recognize areas within the composition which require special attention – rehearsing, where necessary, individual parts separately; perhaps, in the case of a large ensemble, separate small-group rehearsals.
- Balance and blend the various parts in the musical texture.
- Ensure precise ensemble ('togetherness') of the performers, so that they keep in perfect time with each other and maintain precision of attack and balance of tone and volume.
- Accept and consider constructive criticism.
- Always *encourage* performers – never embarrass them in any way.

The lists of suggested pieces at the end of chapters in the students' book are deliberately entitled **Linked Listening** (in preference to 'Further Listening') since some of the pieces might be listened to *during* work on the chapter, to reinforce or further demonstrate certain points. In some instances, one or more items suggested for Linked Listening may spark off further composing ideas.

Interspersed at regular intervals throughout the students' book are double-page spreads displaying visual, and occasionally literary or musical, material. This material links to, and sometimes draws together, elements or concepts explored in preceding chapters, but primarily it is intended to serve – in any interpretation whatsoever – as a stimulus towards Composing or Improvising. Details of items included are given on pages 180–182 of this Resource Book.

IT

It is expected that throughout the course, wherever appropriate, music technology will run alongside. Information technology (IT) is playing an increasingly significant role in music education in helping pupils of all ages and abilities to develop skills in recording, exploring and creating sounds. By bringing electronic equipment into the classroom, pupils can work at their own level to produce either simple, yet effective, responses or sophisticated compositions. It is through this active participation in music making that musical skills and knowledge are developed, together with an appreciation of the physical properties of sound. IT particularly supports pupils with special educational needs by the use of such facilities as a touch screen or Braille keyboard.

Computer programs provide a way in to composing by creating sounds and then organizing them. Importantly, they are able to store the sounds so that they may be saved for future recall, when students may then alter them, refine them, and perhaps enhance them by adding 'live' instrumental and/or vocal parts when playing them back.

Electronic keyboards have also made an impact in the classroom by offering pupils a range of opportunities for composing and performing activities. Pre-set electronic features can encourage a sense of achievement in the less ambitious pupils whereas the wider applications of advanced hardware and software allow the more adventurous to synthesize sounds, arrange and perform music and, in so doing, explore the musical elements. There is a vast choice of equipment these days, including sound modules, samplers, sequencers, synthesizers, MIDI (Musical Instrument Digital Interface) systems, rhythm machines and effects units. Purpose-designed sequencing software converts the computer into a digital recorder and enables compositions to be built up gradually and to be refined, edited and printed. Schools can also benefit greatly from the multi-track recorder for mixing and producing high-quality recordings. Other advantages include the chance to perform differentiated tasks.

IT, therefore, helps to overcome common problems such as poor performances, and pupils are able to tackle activities which were previously too much of a struggle. Musical literacy problems are eased by an IT program which will produce a written version of a pupil's composition. There is much scope for the pupils to make the musical decisions; it is IT that actually opens up these new opportunities for creativity and learning.

Further information on sampling, using a porta-studio, multi-tracking, and using more sophisticated IT (8-track, MIDI, computer, audio-mixer, and timecode) can be found on pages 65–69 of this Resource Book. Using IT in music also links in with the Programme of Study for Key Stage 4 Information Technology.

Notate

Throughout this Teacher's Resource Book, where appropriate to chapter material, there are references to Longman Logotron's computer music program, *Notate*. Many of the 'Using *Notate*' sections are addressed directly to the student – in the event of the teacher photocopying such pages and handing them out. Similarly, many of the *Notate* music printouts could be photocopied and handed out for Performing.

Notate could, in fact, provide ways in for a whole range of students. Some of the ideas presented from page 46 onwards in the *Notate* handbook are musically very simple but may well provide a basic exploration of certain core elements and devices – for example, rhythm (especially), pitch, drone, ostinato. By using *Notate*, students are continually consolidating and widening their knowledge and practical experience of staff notation.

Facility of setting up blue file card icons on the icon bar

Among the utilities supplied with Archimedes is one called *!TinyDirs*. This can be useful when using the *Notate* program.

- Locate *!TinyDirs*, and load. A blue file card icon will appear on the icon bar.
- Now load *!Notate* in the usual way from the *Notate* directory viewer.
- Drag Songs down onto the blue file card icon on the icon bar. The word 'Songs' will appear below the icon.
- Repeat with Voices – dragging the box down over the Songs icon on the icon bar.
- You can also bring down Ideas, Patterns, and Templates, by clicking with *select* on the blue Songs icon on the icon bar, then dragging them down from the Songs directory. Drag each one over an existing blue icon.
- Then all you need to do, at any time, is to click with *select* on a blue icon on the icon bar and its Directory will immediately be displayed.

For more impact, vividness of sound, and truthfulness of timbre, consider connecting the Archimedes computer to an external amplifier – a HiFi or similar. (See 'Hints and Tips', page 57, of the *Notate* handbook.)

Evaluating (Appraising)

Throughout the course, teachers will find many opportunities for students to critically and constructively evaluate their own and others' compositions, and their own and others' performances.

The importance of evaluating cannot be too strongly stressed. It is an essential process and students need to be able to evaluate objectively and critically – whether the work in question is their own, or that of fellow students, or of established composers and performers.

In the case of students' own work, self-evaluation is an ongoing activity. Besides evaluation of the refined, final product there should also be continuous evaluation of the process leading to it:

- evaluating at every possible stage during the creating of a composition ('Is this how I want it to sound?');
- evaluating while practising or rehearsing ('Am I playing/singing the right notes, at the right time, in the right way?').

Possible interpretations of the word evaluate might include: 'determine or assess the value of', 'investigate, and decide the worth of', 'reflect critically and constructively upon'.

Central to all evaluating, of course, is active, critical listening – from which, with increasing experience, knowledge and understanding, will stem informed judgements, decisions, and reasoned argument.

Items from the Linked Listening lists at the end of each chapter in the students' book provide many opportunities for evaluating complete pieces.

Evaluating a composition

Some criteria which may be taken into account when evaluating a composition are given below – and again, in question form, on pages 158 and 159 as copymaster sheets for students. The questions could be answered by students individually, or used as a basis for group discussion. Not all of them will, of course, be appropriate to all compositions, or to all styles or genres. And others, not included here, may be of crucial importance in evaluating certain pieces. For example, in 'experimental' music, some elements mentioned in connection with variety/contrast may need to be replaced by density, articulation, duration, nuance, location.

It has been the intention to formulate the questions in such a way that they will fit whether students are evaluating:

- their own composition;
- a composition by one or more fellow students;
- a composition by an established composer.

Possible criteria:

1. impact and overall impression of the piece; whether it holds the listener's attention
2. variety/contrast – e.g. of dynamics, timbre, pitch, melody, rhythm, texture
3. exploration, appropriate use, and control of musical elements
4. unity – consistency of style
5. form – overall shape, design, structure, organization of ideas
6. effective use of climax
7. originality of ideas – explored, extended, developed, in effective ways
8. choice of medium – instrument(s)/voice(s)/sound-source(s) – used effectively, and with understanding
9. mood and character – appropriateness to the title and/or words of the piece
10. clarity and accuracy of chosen notation; clear performance directions

Also, in the case of students evaluating their own composition, an understanding of the process of how the piece evolved from initial stimuli/ideas to the refined final version, and the ability to describe this.

And, in the case of a group composition, an evaluation of their own individual contribution, and attainment.

Evaluating a performance

Some criteria which may be taken into account when evaluating a performance are given below – and again, in question form, on pages 160–163 as copymaster sheets for students. The questions could be answered by students individually, or used as a basis for group discussion.

It has been the intention to formulate the questions in such a way that they will fit whether students are evaluating:

- their own 'live' performance, from memory of the experience;
- a tape recording of their performance;
- a performance by one or more fellow students, 'live' or taped;
- a performance by one or more professional musicians, 'live' or recorded.

Possible criteria:

1 accuracy of notes/pitch

2 accuracy of rhythm

3 effective use of dynamics

4 use of appropriate tempo

5 control of tempo (whether steady, or changing)

6 suitable qualities and variations of tone/timbre

7 an understanding of the character and style of the music

8 an awareness of the overall shape (form, design, structure) of the piece

9 faithful and sensitive interpretation of the composer's intentions (e.g. with regard to directions of tempo, dynamics, phrasing, other expression markings)

10 a sense of commitment, and involvement with the music

11 effective presentation and communication of the music to the listener

Also, if a vocal performance:

12 breath control

13 clarity of diction

14 expressive interpretation of the mood and meaning of the words

Differentiation

This involves the setting of tasks/questions for different students' needs so that all are able to score positively; and measuring the success (rather than the failure) of all students, each being able to demonstrate what he/she knows, understands, and can do.

Differentiation may be achieved:

- by outcome – presenting the same task to all students, all abilities, and differentiating by outcome; or

- by task – assigning different tasks to different groups of students (or individual students) according to their needs and levels of ability.

It is expected that most of the tasks in the students' book will be challenging enough for students in the middle and upper ability range. However, some students may struggle with a particular element or concept (for example, texture). Some may find some aspects of the work difficult in terms of Performing, Composing, Listening. And some may need other 'ways in' to some of the material, or extension work to develop and consolidate skills, knowledge and understanding.

In some chapters of the students' book – where certain aspects of the work might be too difficult for all – the Composing tasks are gathered together, and headed by a rubric such as 'Try one (or more) or these composing ideas'. Some will be fairly straightforward; others, more taxing and extending.

Mostly, however, Composing tasks have intentionally been worded to be as open-ended as possible, so that students may respond according to their individual levels of ability.

The question sheets for evaluating compositions and performances (copymasters on pages 158–163 of this Resource Book) might be handed out to students for all to evaluate a particular composition or performance – each student responding according to his/her level of ability and musical and critical perception.

The extra, photocopiable, Listening Assignments (pages 165–179) are mainly aimed at students in the D to G grade band.

As mentioned earlier, many of the *Notate* ideas could provide ways in, and opportunities for differentiation by task.

It is hoped that the geographical chart, on the next two pages, will be useful to teachers for 'orientation'. The same goes for the world map on pages 14 and 15, which locates some of the countries/cultures whose musics are represented. The map is reproduced in the students' book, pages 6 and 7.

The music of many of the countries on the chart is described in detail in reference works such as 'The New Grove Dictionary of Music and Musicians' and 'The New Harvard Dictionary of Music' (1986). Background notes on various items of folk and non-Western music included in the students' book and on the compact discs will be found in section 2 of this Resource Book, in the relevant chapters' support materials. Two examples of oriental music notations – Japanese and Chinese – are briefly investigated on pages 97 and 118/119 of the students' book.

Geographical chart of some of the musical cultures of the world

North America

United States of America

Canada

American Indian

The music of the aboriginal peoples (culturally separate) of North, Central, and South America

West Indian

The English-speaking countries of the Caribbean (including Jamaica, Trinidad)

Latin America

South America

Central America and Mexico

The Spanish-speaking countries of the Caribbean (including Cuba)

Australia and Oceania

Oceania is the collective name for the islands of central, south and west Pacific, which form three groups:

Micronesia

Melanesia (including Papua New Guinea)

Polynesia (including Hawaii, Tahiti, New Zealand)

East Asia

China

Japan

Korea

Mongolia

Tibet

South Asia

India

Pakistan

Bangladesh

Nepal

Sri Lanka

Kashmir – which includes parts of India, Pakistan, and China

South-east Asia

Myanmar (Burma)

Thailand

Laos

Kampuchia (Cambodia)

Vietnam*

Philippines

Malaysia

Indonesia (including Bali, Java, Sumatra)

Singapore

(*Although geographically in South-east Asia, Vietnam has strong cultural connections with East Asia, particularly China)

Near East

The musical cultures of West Asia and North Africa, including:

The Arabian Peninsula (including Saudi Arabia, Yemen)

The Arabian Gulf (Kuwait, Bahrain, Qatar, United Arab Emirates)

Iran

Iraq

Turkey

Syria

Lebanon

Jordan

Israel

North Africa – Egypt, Libya, Tunisia, Algeria, Morocco (these last three also known collectively as the Maghrib)

Africa

The musical cultures of Africa south of the southern edge of the Sahara desert (north of that line being counted, musically, as Near East)

Europe	
Albania	Serbia
Andorra	Slovakia
Austria	Slovenia
Belarus	Spain
Belgium	Sweden
Bosnian Croat Federation	Switzerland
Bosnian Serb Republic	Turkey (part)
Bulgaria	Ukraine
Croatia	United Kingdom (England, Scotland, Wales, Northern Ireland)
Czech Republic	The Vatican
Denmark	
Estonia	
Finland	
France	
Germany	
Greece	
Hungary	
Iceland	
Irish Republic	
Italy	
Latvia	
Liechtenstein	
Lithuania	
Luxembourg	
Macedonia	
Moldova	
Monaco	
Netherlands	
Norway	
Poland	
Portugal	
Romania	
Russia (part)	
San Marino	

World Map

80°
160°
140°
120°
100°
80°
60°
40°
20°
0°
ARCTIC
60°
NORWA
BRITISH ISLES
(CANADA)
NORTH AMERICA
40°
UNITED STATES OF AMERICA
Washington
Madrid
SPAIN
NAVAJO TERRITORY
ATLANTIC OCEAN
20°
NORTHER
Sahar
CARIBBEAN
PACIFIC OCEAN
0°
SOUTH AMERICA
La Paz
BOLIVIA
TAHITI
20°
CHILE
Santiago
40°
160°
140°
120°
100°
80°
60°
40°
20°
0°
This map shows some of the countries/cultures whose musics are represented in this course.

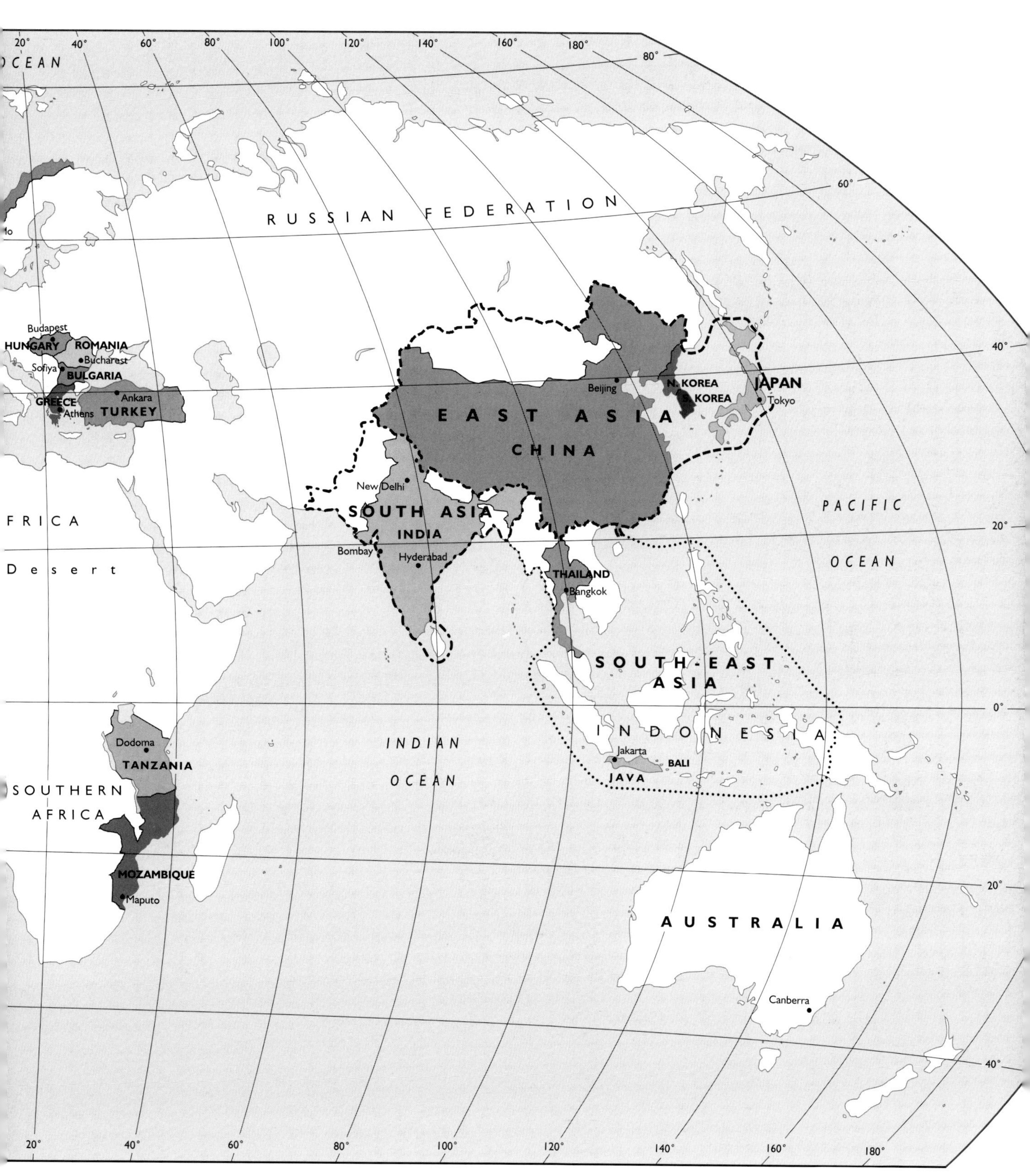

OCEAN
RUSSIAN FEDERATION
Budapest
HUNGARY
ROMANIA
Bucharest
Sofiya
BULGARIA
GREECE
Athens
Ankara
TURKEY
EAST ASIA
CHINA
Beijing
N. KOREA
S. KOREA
JAPAN
Tokyo
New Delhi
SOUTH ASIA
INDIA
Bombay
Hyderabad
FRICA
Desert
THAILAND
Bangkok
PACIFIC
OCEAN
SOUTH-EAST ASIA
INDONESIA
Jakarta
BALI
JAVA
INDIAN
OCEAN
Dodoma
TANZANIA
SOUTHERN
AFRICA
MOZAMBIQUE
Maputo
AUSTRALIA
Canberra

Possible schemes of work

Scheme 1				Scheme 2
Year 9: 5 half terms, 2 chapters per half term	1	Rhythm (1)	page 19	Year 10: 6 half terms, 3 chapters per half term
	2	Shaping melodies	27	
	3	Timbre (1)	30	
	4	Tempo and dynamics – expressive effects	34	
	5	Major, minor, and pentatonic	38	
	6	Music with a drone	44	
	7	Chords and chord patterns	52	
	8	Graphic notation	57	
	9	Ternary form	58	
	10	Using ostinatos	62	
Year 10: 6 half terms, 2 chapters per half term	11	Some musical devices	73	
	12	Mood and character	76	
	13	Texture	80	
	14	Rondo form	87	
	15	Programme music	89	
	16	Timbre (2) – New sounds, new colours	95	
	17	Words and music	97	
	18	Making comparisons	103	
	19	Rhythm (2)	111	Year 11: 4 half terms, 3 chapters per half term
	20	Chords and clusters	114	
	21	Music as background to words	120	
	22	Tension – and release	122	
Year 11: 4 half terms, 2 chapters per half term	23	More musical devices	126	
	24	Variations	137	
	25	Chromatic, whole-tone, and modal	139	
	26	Timbre (3) – Exploring the voice	146	
	27	Making use of physical space	149	
	28	Tonal and atonal	151	
	29	Chance and choice – aleatory music	154	
	30	Mixed media, and the theatre element	155	

A possible strategy for creating a piece of music

Annotated version of the flow chart (algorithm) 'A possible strategy for creating a piece of music', printed on page 8 of the students' book

1 Experimenting/exploring ideas and possibilities, deciding on the type of sound-source(s) and the kinds of sounds to be used

2 Selecting those most suitable; rejecting others

3 Composing, building up, the piece – continuously evaluating (some students may, of course, notate as they compose)

4 If working in a group leading to performance, the piece will need to be rehearsed; an individual performance will require practise

5 Recording a performance of the piece

6 Listening to the recording and appraising the piece – discussing and evaluating the composition (and perhaps also the performance and the quality of the recording)

7 Evaluating will probably lead to adjusting, refining – and re-recording

8 Choosing the most appropriate way to notate the music, making it as clear and accurate as possible

9 Writing or recording a commentary, describing how the piece evolved from initial stimuli / ideas to the refined final version

10 Storing the refined end-product safely – notated, and /or recorded, or stored in a computer

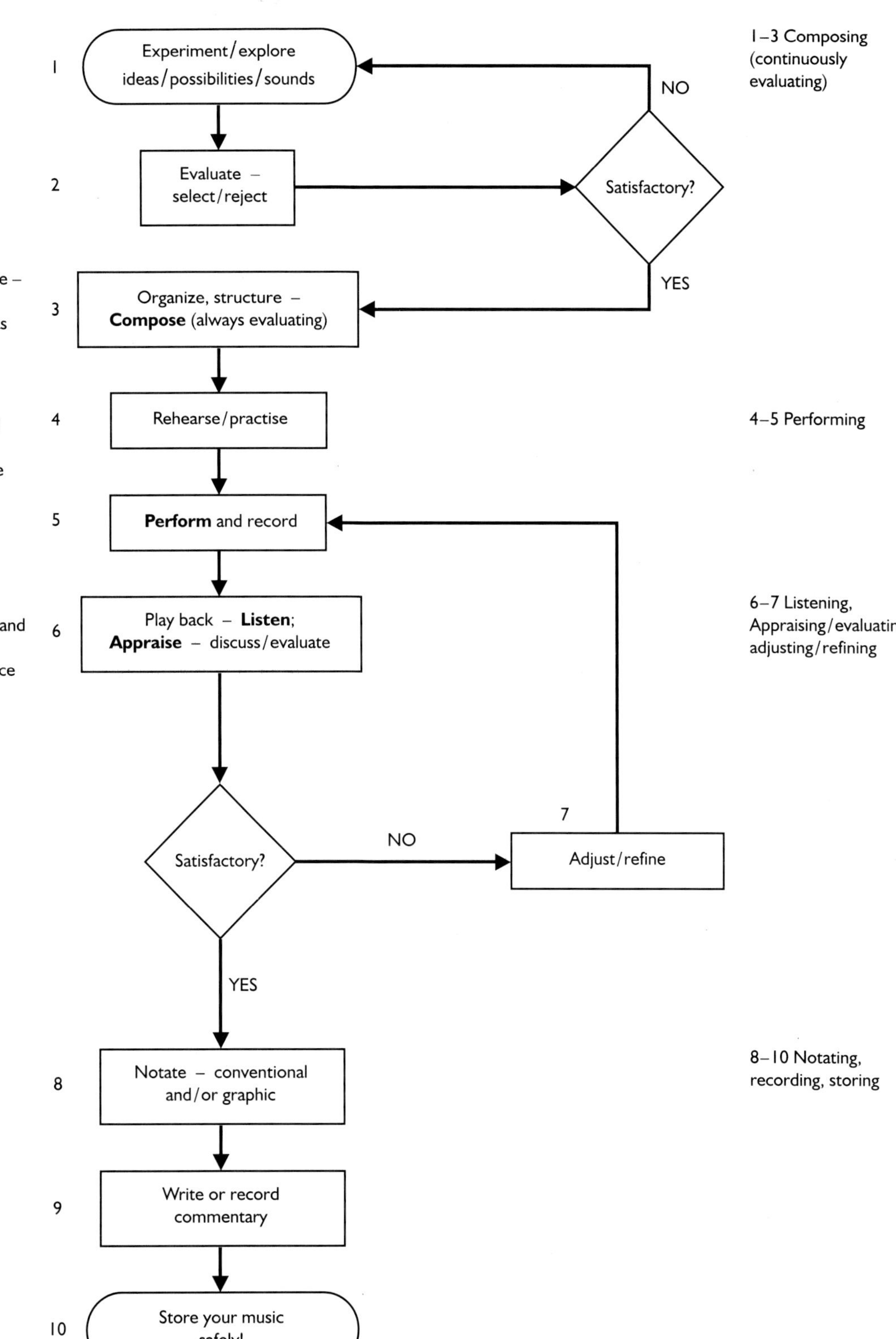

Chapter by chapter support materials

This section of the Resource Book consists of the following materials – arranged throughout, chapter by chapter, page by page, to match the students' book.

- Answers to questions in the students' book.
- Opportunities for using *Notate.*
- Background notes on items of folk and non-Western music included in the students' book.
- Other background information, and suggestions.
- Linked Listening – recordings on other cassettes.
- *Notate* music printouts.
- Answers to the copymaster Listening Assignments.

All page numbers printed in the margins refer to the relevant pages in the students' book.

CHAPTER 1 Rhythm (1)

Students' book: pages 9–16

Summary of students' material

beat, pulse

grouping of beats to make a repeating pattern

time/metre

bars and bar-lines

accent and non-accent

duple, triple, quadruple metres

time signature

$\frac{2}{4}$ $\frac{3}{4}$ $\frac{4}{4}$

rhythm

characterized by accent and non-accent, duration – and silence

notes and rests (chart)

time-values of notes in relation to the semibreve (chart)

simple time signatures (chart)

Composer	Music	Genre/form/style	Culture/country of origin
CD 1.1 Moon Pyung Hwang	*Tiger Dance*	dance in folk style	Korea
CD 1.2 Bizet	*Prelude to Carmen*	operatic prelude	France
CD 1.3 Level 42	*Running in the Family*	rock song	England

Page 9 Background notes on the *Tiger Dance*, from Korea

- Korean music can be classified according to five categories: court music (*aak*), ritual (other than court music), vocal art music, folk (*minsogak*), and 'new compositions'.
- The music is a blend of Chinese ingredients and native Korean ingredients.
- Instruments are classified according to eight categories (originating in the Chinese court): metal, stone, silk, bamboo, gourd, clay, skin, wood. (This is based on the Confucian idea that 'the world will be at peace when these materials are in harmony'.)
- Most Korean music is in triple metre – but duple metre is quite common in folk-music.
- The basic Korean instrumental ensemble consists of *hyangp'iri* (double-reed wind instrument), *taegŭm* (bamboo flute), *haegŭm* (two-string fiddle), and *changgo* (hour-glass drum). For *Tiger Dance*, Moon Pyung Hwang adds other drums, cymbals and gong.
- There are eight distinct types of notation for Korean music – each performing a different function.

Page 12 **Answer** (Listening)

The bass guitar (played by Mark King, voted 'the best bassist in the world') is moving along freely in rhythm.

Page 12 **Using *Notate***

Ideas in the *Notate* handbook (page 47) might link to the work on this page:
'Exploring pulse (3)'
'Dividing the beat into 2'
'Dividing the beat into 4'

Page 14 **Using *Notate***

It is possible to write a score of the rhythm round quite quickly on *Notate*, using the Copy facility. Page 22 of this Resource Book could be photocopied and handed out to students for them to follow the instructions, and then print out copies for performance. Or, pages 23 to 25 could be photocopied and handed out for immediate performance.

Page 14 **Using *Notate***

'Using the same rhythms together' on page 48 of the *Notate* handbook could provide a further or alternative Composing activity.

Page 15 **Answers** (Listening)

1 $\frac{2}{4}$ (duple)

2 The 'gaps' are not of the same length:

hyangp'iri – 4 bars
taegŭm – 6 bars
haegŭm – 4 bars
cymbals – 2 bars

Page 16 Linked listening – recordings on cassettes

Item	Cassette
Sousa: March – *The Stars and Stripes Forever* (arranged Bob Sharples)	'Adventures in Music' Book 4
Richard Rodgers: *March of the Siamese Children*	'Adventures in Music' Book 4
Encina: *Triste España*	'Enjoying Early Music'
Haydn: Minuet from Symphony No. 6 in D (*Le Matin*)	'Score-reading'
Haydn: Minuet from String Quartet in B♭, Opus 50 No. 1	'Investigating Musical Styles', cassette 2 item 55
Mozart: Minuet from *Eine kleine Nachtmusik*	'Form and Design', cassette 2
Mozart: Minuet from Divertimento No. 1 in E♭ (K113)	'New Assignments and Practice Scores', Score 7
Mozart: Minuet from Symphony No. 36 in C (The 'Linz')	'Musical Forms: Listening Scores'
Beethoven: Minuet from Septet in E♭	'Form and Design', cassette 2
Khatchaturian: *Sabre Dance*	'Adventures in Music' Book 2
Lecuona: *Malagueña* and *Danza lucumí*	'Adventures in Music' Book 3
Varèse: *Ionisation*	'Enjoying Modern Music'
African percussion rhythms	'Investigating Musical Styles', cassette 1 item 14
Balinese gamelan music	'Adventures in Music' Book 4

Page 14 Using *Notate*

Rhythm Round

It is possible to write a score of the rhythm round quite quickly on *Notate*, using the Copy facility.

- Open up a window, and set up four percussion tracks.
- Write the four-bar rhythm (page 14) in track 1. You will, however, need to write ♪♪♪ instead of the triplet (♪♪♪) in bar 3.
- Now highlight the four-bar rhythm as a grey block – move the mouse pointer to the left of the first note, press and hold down *select* and drag the pointer to the right until you include the last note. Release *select*. Click with *menu* and move the pointer to the word Edit. Pass right, highlighting the word Copy in black, and click with *select*. Move the insert pointer to the beginning of bar 5 of track 1 and click with *select*. Bars 1–4 will be copied into bars 5–8. Click again with select to remove the highlight.
- Highlight bars 1–8 of track 1 and copy them, in the same way, into bars 9–16. Add a double bar (‖) at the end of bar 16.
- Highlight all but the last bar of track 1 as a grey block. Copy this into track 2 – beginning at bar 2.
- Highlight all but the last bar of track 2, and copy this into track 3 – beginning at bar 3.
- In the same way, copy all but the last bar of track 3 into track 4 – beginning at bar 4.
- Add a semibreve rest (–) to each of the six empty bars at the beginning of the piece.
- Decide whether to adjust the last half of bar 16 in tracks 2, 3 and 4 to be a minim (as track 1) so that all four parts will end up neatly and together.
- Play back the rhythm round – the voice on each track will be Percussion-Soft. Now select four very different percussion voices, and play back again. Which version sounds most effective? Why?
- The tempo setting is ♩= 120. Try a different tempo – e.g. ♩ = 108, then ♩ = 84. Which tempo suits the music best?

Alternatively, the rhythm round could be notated on one of the percussion Template files in the *Notate* Songs directory – e.g. Perc2, which has four percussion tracks already set up for (1) TomTom, (2) Claves 1, (3) Clap, (4) CowBell.

After notating the rhythm round, print out copies, and perform it in a group of four musicians, each with a contrasting percussion instrument.

Rhythm Round

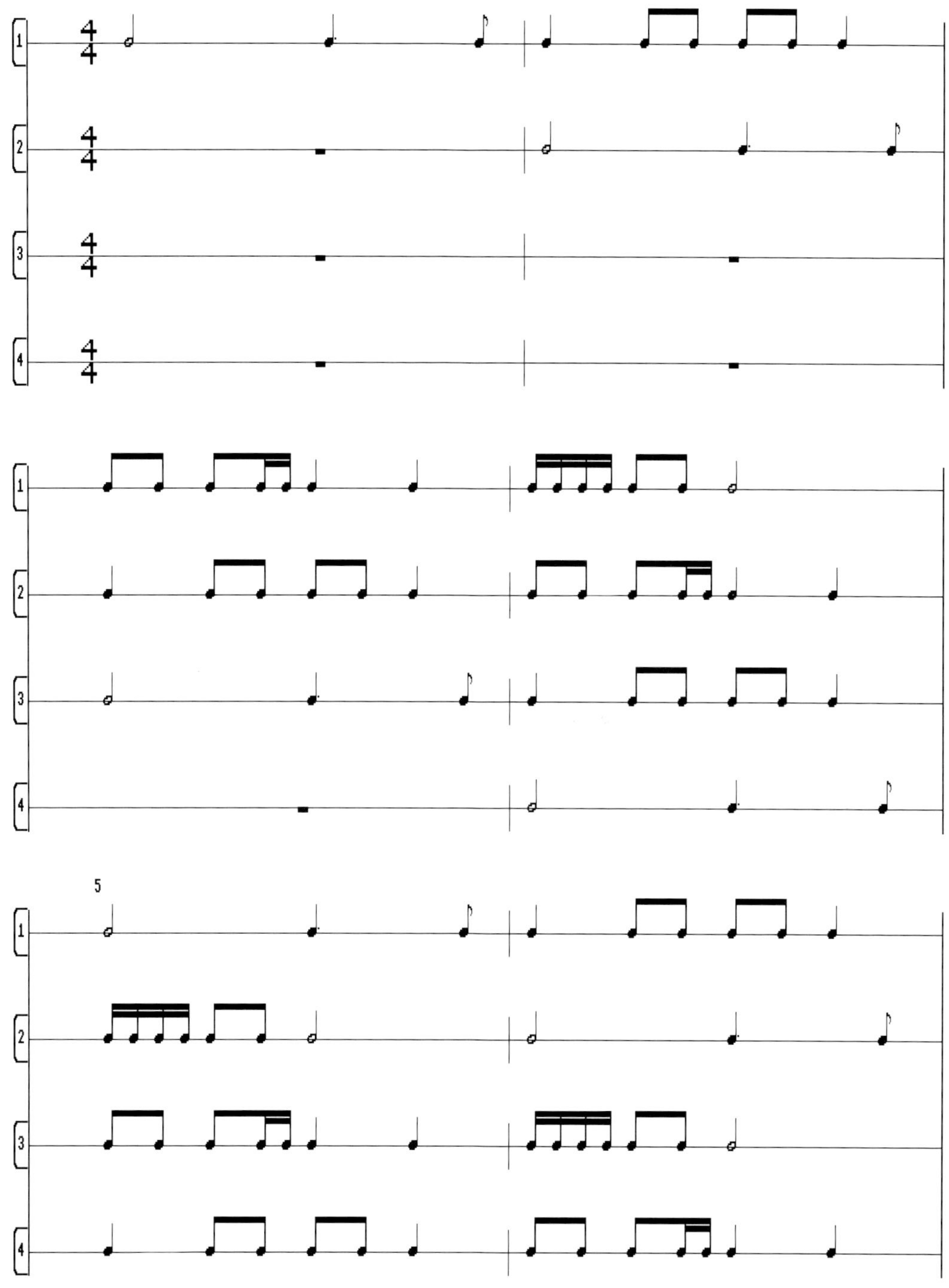

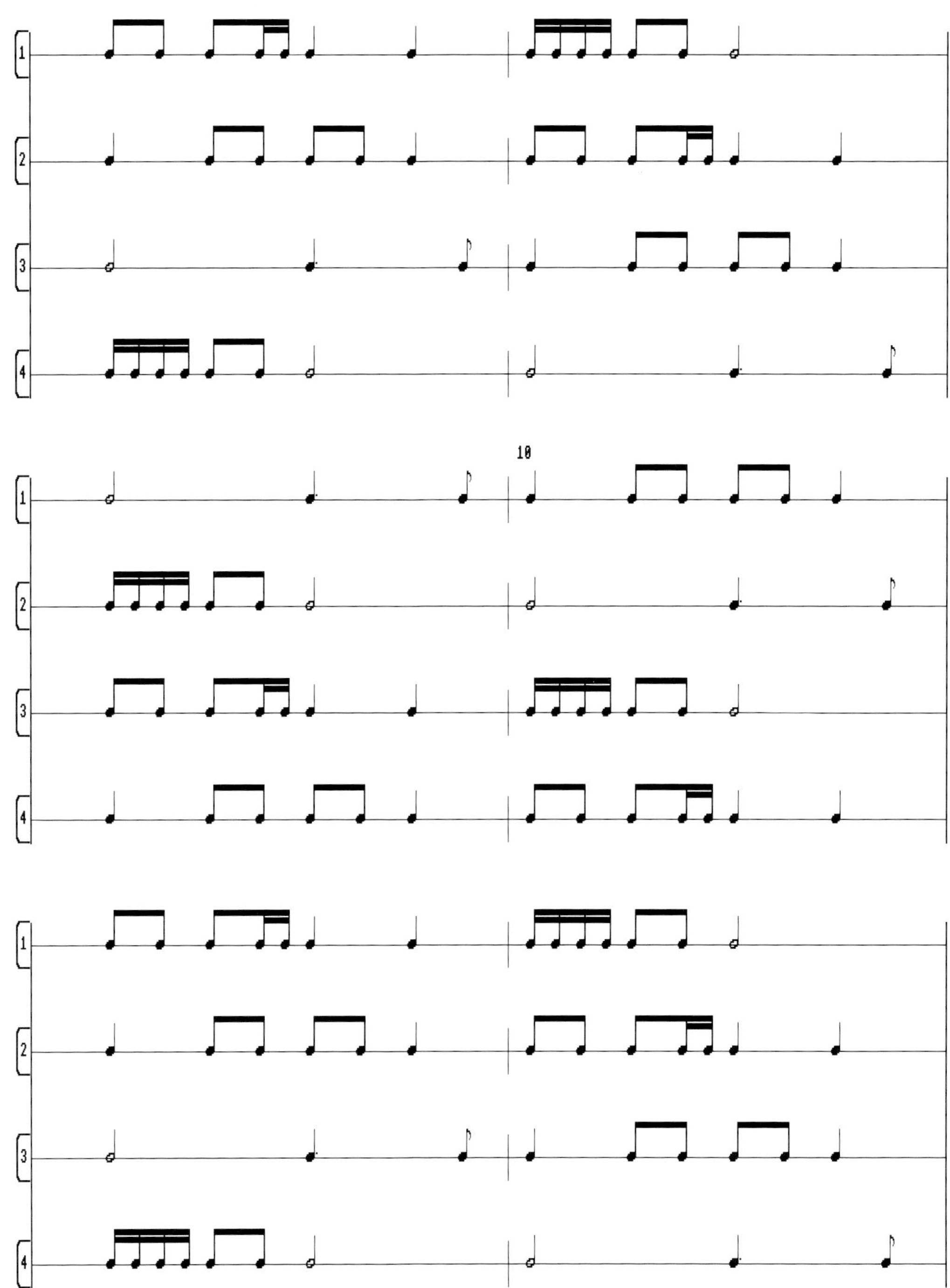
1
2
3
4
10

1
2
3
4
15
1
2
3
4

Listening Assignment A

Answers

Extract from Prelude to the opera *Carmen* by Bizet

1 The instruments you hear first are:

woodwind ☐ brass ☑ percussion ☐

2 Then the tune is played by:

violins ☑ trumpets ☐ clarinets ☐

3 The music is in the style of:

a waltz ☐ a march ☑ a jig ☐

4 The tune is played again – with the full orchestra joining in. The tune is now played:

(a) higher than before ☑ lower than before ☐

and (b) more quietly ☐ more loudly ☑

5 You now hear a different tune. Two percussion instruments which add excitement and brilliance to the music are:

(a) cymbals

(b) triangle

6 At the end of the piece, the music:

slows down ☐ gets quicker ☐ keeps the same speed ☑

7 The mood of this music is:

dreamy ☐ solemn ☐ joyful ☑ mysterious ☐

8 What do you like, or dislike, about this music?

(personal response – expressing and justifying opinion/preference)

CHAPTER 2 Shaping melodies

Students' book: pages 17–23

Summary of students' material

melody
shape/contour
melodic movement by step
phrases and phrase-marks
range
octave
movement by leap
movement by balanced mixture of step and leap, with some repeated notes
tie
repetition
varied repetition
clefs – treble and bass
pitches on bass and treble clefs related to lettered keys on keyboard
characteristic features of a melody (chart)
unity, variety
strict time, free time
comparing melodies from different cultures

Composer	Music	Genre/form/style	Culture/country of origin
———	*O Waly, Waly*	folk-song	Scotland and England
CD Strauss II	*The Blue Danube*	concert waltz	Austria
CD 1.4 Gershwin	*Bess, You is My Woman Now* from *Porgy and Bess*	song from an opera	USA
CD 1.5 Dvořák	melody from the slow movement of Symphony No. 9 *(From the New World)*	symphony	Bohemia (now Czech Republic)
———	*Dance*	traditional dance	Tanzania (East Africa)
———	*Lotus Blossoms*	traditional melody	China
———	*Little Father Horse-washer*	folk-song	Java
———	*Weaving Dance*	folk-dance	India
———	*Happy Song*	traditional song	Navajo (North American Indian)
———	*The Bold Hussar*	folk-song	Hungary

Page 17 *O, Waly, Waly*

⌴ = notes immediately repeated
‿ = notes moving by step

Page 18 **Answers** (Performing)

1 Bars 2, 6, 10, 14

2 Bars 4, 8, 12

3 Bars 8 and 12

4 Bar 7

Answer (Listening)

Porgy sings a leap of a 9th in bars 12–13 and 16–17.

Page 19 **Answers**

On the third beat of bar 9, straight quavers (♫) instead of dotted quaver plus semiquaver (♪.♬)

Other repetitions:
bar 10 – repetition of bar 2;
bar 13 – repetition of bar 12.

Other varied repetitions:
bar 6 could be counted as a varied repetition of bar 5;
bar 11 could be counted as a varied repetition of bar 1 – with the last three notes now backwards, and an octave higher;
bars 14 and 15 are a varied repetition of bar 13, with the note values doubled in length (in augmentation).

Page 22 **Using *Notate***

Ideas Nos. 4 and 5 could be composed using *Notate* – then the music saved and/or printed out for performance.

Page 23 Linked listening – recordings on cassettes

Item	Cassette
Plainchant: *Hodie Christus natus est*	'Enjoying Early Music'
Beethoven: theme from last movement of Symphony No. 9 ('Choral')	'Score-reading', two extracts
Pugnani, arranged Kreisler: *Praeludium*	'Score-reading'
Wagner: *The Ride of the Valkyries*	'Enjoying Music' Book 1
Mozart: *Lacrymosa* from the Requiem	'Musical Forms: Listening Scores'
Brahms: Hungarian Dance No. 5	'Form and Design', cassette 2
Prokofiev: *Montagues and Capulets* from *Romeo and Juliet*	'Musical Forms: Listening Scores'
Prokofiev: Gavotte from the *Classical Symphony*	'Discovering Music' Book 1; 'Form and Design', cassette 2
Schoenberg: Theme from *Variations for Orchestra*	'Enjoying Modern Music'
Khatchaturian: *Sabre Dance*	'Adventures in Music' Book 2

CHAPTER 3 Timbre (1)

Students' book: pages 24–31

Summary of students' material

timbre/tone-quality/tone colour
factors determining the timbre of an instrument
harmonics, harmonic series
comparing timbres of various instruments of the orchestra
investigating the distinctive timbres of an ensemble from Thailand
varying the timbre of an instrument
contrasting timbres in a piece by Walton and in a piece of swing
32-bar pattern: A A B A
synaesthesia

Composer	Music	Genre/form/style	Culture/country of origin
CD 1.6 ———	note A above middle C played by three different instruments	———	———
Rimsky-Korsakov	*Scena* and the first part of *Canto gitano* (Gypsy Song) from *Spanish Caprice*	orchestral suite	Russia
CD 1.7 Pichit Paiboon	*Ricebowl*	descriptive piece in folk style	Thailand
CD 1.8 Walton	*Popular Song* from *Façade*	orchestral suite	England
CD 1.9 Benny Goodman	*Stompin' at the Savoy*	jazz, swing	USA
Scelsi	*Quattro Pezzi* (Four Pieces)	pieces for orchestra	Italy
Bartók	*Giuoco delle coppie* (The game of the couples) from *Concerto for Orchestra*	concerto for orchestra	Hungary

Page 24 **Answer** (Listening)

Violin, trumpet, clarinet

Page 25 *Scene* from *Spanish Caprice* – a single-line score, showing the essential musical information, is printed on page 19 of 'Enjoying Music' Book 2.

Page 26 Background notes on *Ricebowl*, from Thailand

- Thai music has been strongly influenced by the musical cultures of China and India.
- Thai music is basically pentatonic – five pitches are chosen from seven equidistant pitches.
- There is a great deal of melodic repetition, often with much ornamentation. The music is almost always in $\frac{2}{4}$ time.
- *Ricebowl* is performed by the most typical Thai ensemble, called *pi phat* – named after its main instrument, the *pi nai* (large shawm with quadruple reed).
- The distinctive timbre of the *pi nai* is often heard in the background during Thai kick boxing and Muay Thai contests regularly screened on satellite television.

Page 27 Composing

Students might notate their piece in the form of a graphic score, with an explanatory key.

Page 28 Although nicknamed 'The King of Swing', Benny Goodman (1909–1986) also earned himself a reputation as a performer of classical music – the first jazz musician to do so. In 1938 he recorded Mozart's Clarinet Quintet with the Budapest String Quartet. The same year, he commissioned Bartók's *Contrasts* for violin, clarinet and piano. Bartók was still living in Budapest at the time, but visited the USA in 1940 when he recorded the work with Goodman and Szigeti (a recording currently available on CD). Other Goodman recordings of classical music included Mozart's Clarinet Concerto, Copland's Clarinet Concerto (commissioned by Goodman), Stravinsky's *Ebony Concerto*, and chamber works by Beethoven, Brahms, Poulenc, and Weber.

Page 30 *Giuoco delle coppie* from Bartók's Concerto for Orchestra is recorded on 'Instruments of the Orchestra', cassette 2.

Bartók features instruments as follows:

> Rhythmic introduction, featuring snare drum (with the snares lifted away from the skin), leading into:
>
> Section A^1: the 'couples'
> two bassoons (playing in 6ths), two oboes (in 3rds), two clarinets (in 7ths), two flutes (in 5ths), two muted trumpets (in 2nds).
>
> Snare drum leads into:
>
> Section B: brass (four horns, three trumpets, two trombones and tuba) + snare drum.
>
> Section A^2: two bassoons (now plus a third bassoon), two oboes (now plus clarinets), clarinets (helped by flutes), flutes (now with oboes, clarinets and bassoons), muted trumpets (now with two harps added to the string accompaniment).

The piece is structured in ternary form (A^1 B A^2), 'threaded through' with rhythms on snare drum. The complete structure is:

Introduction:	snare drum
A^1:	featuring the 'couples' – successive pairs of woodwind instruments
Link:	snare drum
B:	a contrast, featuring the brass section playing a solemn chorale, with rhythmic patterns on snare drum
Link:	snare drum + woodwinds
A^2:	featuring the 'couples' again – but now varied by the addition of extra strands of colourful timbres
Coda	swiftly-repeated woodwind chords, + snare drum

Answer (Composing)

Bartók brings out the structure of the piece by using timbre to achieve *balance* (the 'couples' featured in A^1 return in A^2 and in the same order), and *contrast* and *variety* (between the 'couples' – and especially the contrast presented by the timbres of the brass in section B). *Unity* is achieved by the timbre of the snare drum 'threading through' the whole structure.

Page 31 Linked listening – recordings on cassettes

Item	Cassette
Britten: *The Young Person's Guide to the Orchestra*	'Instruments of the Orchestra', cassette 2, conducted by Britten (the work is recorded in separate sections throughout the cassette)
Delius: Prelude to *Irmelin*	'Instruments of the Orchestra', cassette 2
Debussy: *Prélude à l'après-midi d'un faune*	'Enjoying Modern Music'
Webern: No. 1 of *Five Movements for Strings*, Opus 5	'New Assignments and Practice Scores', cassette 2 item 6
Webern: No. 3 of *Five Pieces for Orchestra*, Opus 10	'New Assignments and Practice Scores', Score 12
Copland: *Hoe-down* from *Rodeo*	'Adventures in Music: Ballet'
Copland: *Variations on a Shaker Song* from *Appalachian Spring*	'Discovering Music' Book 1

CHAPTER 4 Tempo and dynamics – expressive effects

Students' book: pages 34–41

Summary of students' material

performance directions – tempo marking, dynamic markings
phrase relationship
expression markings
tempo markings (chart)
markings for changes of tempo (chart)
dynamic markings (chart)
expression markings for articulation (chart)
contrasts of tempo and dynamics in Balinese gamelan music
Italian terms indicating style, mood, and expression (chart)

Composer	Music	Genre/form/style	Culture/country of origin
CD 1.10 Vivaldi	opening of *Autumn* from *The Four Seasons*	violin concerto	Italy
CD 1.11 Wayan Udayana	*Desa Life*	programmatic piece for gamelan	Bali
Orff	*Tempus est iocundum* from *Carmina burana*	a 'scenic cantata'	Germany

Page 34 **Answers** (Listening)

Phrase 2 is the same melody as phrase 1 – but played an octave lower, and *piano* instead of *forte*.

Phrase 4 is a repetition of the last part of phrase 3 – but played an octave lower, *piano* instead of *forte*, beginning on the third beat instead of the first, and with the final note falling to F instead of rising to A.

Page 38 Background notes on the Balinese gamelan piece, *Desa Life*

- *Gamelan* (originally meaning 'to handle bronze') is the general name for an Indonesian orchestra or instrumental ensemble (e.g. from Bali or Java). Instruments most often included are:

  metallophones, of two types: *saron*, and *gĕnder* (similar to a xylophone);

  suspended and horizontal tuned gongs, of different sizes and pitches;

  gong-chimes (sets of knobbed gong kettles) of two main kinds: *trompong*, and *reyong*;

  double-headed drums: *kĕndang*; and cymbals: *ceng-ceng*.

  Also sometimes included are: *suling*, an end-blown bamboo flute; *rabāb*, a two-string spike fiddle; and *guntang*, a one-string bamboo tube zither; also, singers.

- A gamelan is often made up of fifteen to twenty players. There is no conductor; the drummers lead the ensemble and give musical signals (cues) to indicate changes in tempo and dynamic level.
- The music is based on the principle of heterophony. There is a main, fixed melody – known in Bali as *pokok* ('fixed' melody, or 'nuclear' melody). This is played in long notes on lower-sounding instruments and punctuated by the large gongs. Above and around this, other instruments weave decorated versions of the same melody, building up a complicated, continuously changing web of sound made up of inter-locking patterns. In general, the higher the pitch of an instrument, the more notes it contributes to the musical texture.
- The gamelan is revered by all Indonesians; its music expresses their deepest feelings and beliefs. Every village has at least one gamelan, and no two are tuned exactly alike. The instruments are treated with the greatest respect, and are believed to have 'spiritual, charismatic power'. Regular offerings are made to gamelan of incense and flowers.
- Gamelan music is used for entertainment, and as an accompaniment to religious and ceremonial rituals, dance, drama, performances of sung poetry, and shadow puppet plays.
- *Desa Life* is based on a Balinese pentatonic scale called *sĕlisir* – shown here with approximate pitches, which may be called by name or number:

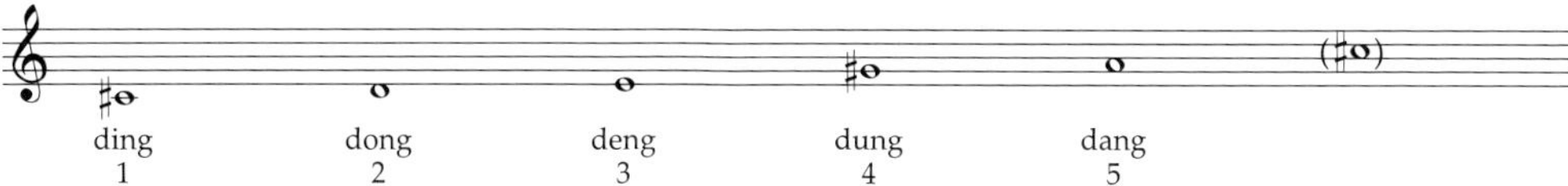

Page 40 Answers (Listening)

1 Orff emphasizes contrasts between *f* and *p* by alternating several bright-sounding percussion instruments played loudly with fewer instruments played less loudly.

2 At the very end of each chorus (in most recordings) there is a pause (silence).

3 Excitement is built up during the music of each verse by an *accelerando* (gradually getting faster), emphasized by the (mainly off-beat) rhythm on castanets, and ending with a *forte* outburst from the choir.

Pages 40/41 Composing

The *Chiaroscuro* composition could be notated in the form of a graphic score, including expression markings, and an explanatory key.

Listening Assignment B

Answers

Swaz hie gat umbe and *Chume, chum geselle min* from *Carmina burana* by Carl Orff

These two songs are for two groups of voices – women's voices, and men's voices. The accompaniment is for orchestra.

Carl Orff makes effective use of repetition and contrast. The music of the first half of Song 2 is repeated for the second half. After Song 2, there is a repeat of Song 1. There are strong musical contrasts between the two songs.

Song 1

At first, the two groups of voices swiftly alternate.

(a) The first group of voices you hear are:

women's voices ☐ men's voices ☑

(b) The second group of voices:

repeats the music of the first group ☑ sings completely different music ☐

(c) Two percussion instruments which add colour and excitement to the last part of Song 1 are:

(1) cymbals

(2) tambourine

Song 2

(d) The first voices you hear are:

women's voices ☑ men's voices ☐

(e) They are singing:

in unison ☑ in two parts ☐

(f) Next to sing are:

women only ☐ men only ☑ men and women together ☐

(g) They are singing:

in unison ☐ in harmony ☑

(Questions continued on sheet 2)

(h) Name the instrument which plays a solo when the singing stops.

flute

(i) The music of Song 2 is:

faster than Song 1 ☐ slower than Song 1 ☑

(j) The dynamic level is:

quieter than Song 1 ☑ louder than Song 1 ☐

(k) The music of Song 2 has:

2 beats to a bar ☐ 3 beats to a bar ☑ 5 beats to a bar ☐

Repeat of Song 1

(1) The tempo of Song 1 is:

moderate ☐ fairly fast ☐ very fast ☑

(m) Just after the women and men start to sing *together*, the music:

slows down for a moment ☑ gets very much faster ☐

(n) A dynamic marking for this song would be:

p ☐ ***mp*** ☐ ***mf*** ☐ ***ff*** ☑

(o) A performance of these two songs creates this musical form:

A Song 1	**B** Song 2 (contrast)	**A** Song 1 (repeated)

The name given to this musical form is: ternary form

(p) Which of the two songs do you like best? Why?

(personal response – expressing and justifying opinion/preference)

CHAPTER 5 Major, minor, and pentatonic

Students' book: pages 42–47

Summary of students' material

repeat signs
major key, minor key
major scale
tones and semitones
pattern of tones and semitones in the major scale
minor scale
key signature
naming the notes/degrees of the scale (chart)
key signatures (chart)
intervals (chart)
major into minor
pentatonic scales

Composer	Music	Genre/form/style	Culture/country of origin
Mozart	*Ah, vous dirai-je, maman* (brief extracts)	variation	Austria
———	*Frère Jacques*	round	France
Mahler	opening of third movement of Symphony No. 1	symphony	Austria
CD 1.12 Dvořák	Slavonic Dance No. 8	dance in folk style	Bohemia (now Czech Republic)
CD 1.13 Lennon and McCartney	*The Fool on the Hill*	orchestral arrangement of a pop song	England
CD 1.14 ———	*Achachikala*	folk-dance	Bolivia

Page 45 The French words of *Frère Jacques* are:

Frère Jacques, Frère Jacques,
Dormez-vous, dormez-vous?
Sonnez les matines, sonnez les matines,
Ding dang dong, ding dang dong.

Page 45 Using *Notate*

Changing *Frère Jacques* into the minor key can be worked on *Notate*, using the song 'Brother' in the *Notate* Songs directory. Page 41 of this Resource Book could be photocopied and handed out to students for them to follow the instructions. Page 42 shows the resulting printout.

Page 45 **Sample answers** (Performing and Listening)

'The tune now sounds sad', 'unhappy', 'mournful'; 'it makes the tune sound a bit sinister'.

Page 45 Third movement of Mahler's Symphony No. 1 in D

This movement of the Symphony was inspired by a satirical drawing by the French engraver, Jacques Callot, of an animals' funeral procession. Stags carry the coffin, upon which sits a fox. Hares gleefully wave flags. There is a band of musicians made up of cats, frogs and crows, and other birds fly above. The grave-digger is a boar. The corpse inside the coffin is that of a hunter . . .

The first part of the movement is based on a two-note ostinato (the notes D and A) first played on kettle drums. Above this, *Frère Jacques*, transformed into the minor, is played in canon. The order in which instruments enter with the tune is:

(a) solo double bass (muted)

(b) bassoon

(c) muted cellos

(d) bass tuba

(e) clarinet and bassoon

(f) muted violas and cellos

(g) horn

(h) four flutes

(i) cor anglais, two clarinets, bass clarinet, and two bassoons

(j) violas and cellos (both divided)

(k) four muted horns and harp

This extract of the movement is recorded on 'New Assignments and Practice Scores', cassette 1 item 22.

Page 45 **Answers** (Listening)

G minor

Major

Page 46 Background notes on *Achachikala*, folk-dance from Bolivia

- Most of the folk-music of Bolivia, like that of the Andes in general, is pentatonic (the origins dating back to the influence of Inca music, whose main musical characteristic was pentatonicism).
- Ensembles almost always include the drum. Drums are believed to have special powers, manifested by the sounds they make as they are struck.
- The *quena* (notched end-blown flute) was the most important wind instrument in pre-Columbian times. It is made of clay, gold, silver, bone, gourd, or (most often now) of cane. Though used for pentatonic melodies, it is in fact capable of producing a two-octave chromatic scale.
- The *charango* is similar to a small Spanish guitar, but has ten strings. The back of the instrument is sometimes made of wood – though more often from a dried armadillo shell, shaped into a figure-of-eight.

Page 47 Linked listening – recordings on cassettes

Item	Cassette
Beethoven: Scherzo and Trio from Piano Sonata No. 2 in A major	'Musical Forms: Listening Scores'
Schubert: *Der stürmische Morgen* from *Winterreise*	'Investigating Musical Styles', cassette 3 item 65
Brahms: Hungarian Dance No. 5	'Form and Design', cassette 2
Bix Beiderbecke: *At the Jazz Band Ball*	'Investigating Musical Styles', cassette 3 item 90
Stravinsky: *Chinese March* from *The Song of the Nightingale*	'Investigating Musical Styles' cassette 1 item 32 (at around 2'24")

Page 45 Using *Notate*

Frère Jacques

- Load the song 'Brother' (which is the round, '*Frère Jacques*') from the *Notate* Songs directory.

- The music is written in the key of C major. Play the song through.

- Now edit the song – first by changing it from C major to C minor. Hold down Ctrl on the keyboard and press F8 to open up the Key Signature dialogue box. With the mouse, click with *select* on Minor, and Flats, and then click three times on the right-hand Flats arrow. Click on OK.

- Play the song. What about tempo? Experiment, and find a tempo which you think suits this minor key version of the song.

- Try changing the voice (instrument) on track 2 (e.g. to vibraphone). Can you hear the two parts in the round more clearly with two *different* voices?

- Now add a track 3, with treble clef (hold down Ctrl and press F5). Starting at the *end* of the song, highlight the whole of track 2 as a grey block – move the mouse pointer to the right of the last note. Press and hold down *select* and drag the pointer to the left until you reach the beginning. Release *select*. Click with *menu* and move the pointer to the word Edit. Pass right, highlighting the word Copy in black, and click with *select*. Move the insert pointer to the beginning of bar 5 of track 3 and click with *select*. The tune will be copied into track 3. Click with *select* to remove the highlight.

- Select a suitable voice for track 3. Play the song. Do all three parts in the round stand out clearly?

- If you wish to, save your edited version of the song. Click with *menu* and move the pointer to the word File. Pass right and move past Save until the 'save as' window appears. Delete the word 'Brother' (only) and type in a title of your own. Click on OK.

Frère Jacques

Listening Assignment C

Answers

The Fool on the Hill by Lennon and McCartney

(CD item 1.13 – consisting of two verses of the song)

1 The melody is first played on:

piccolo ☑ clarinet ☐

alto saxophone ☐ horn ☐

2 The number of beats to a bar is:

two ☑ three ☐ five ☐

3 Listen for the music to slip from major into minor. What particular sound emphasizes the effect?

a (minor) chord on (muted) brass

4 When the music slips back into the major, you hear:

a rising major scale ☐ steadily repeated major chords ☑

5 At the beginning of verse 2, the melody is played by:

violins

6 A suitable dynamic marking for the music would be:

f (forte)

7 In the second (minor key) part of each verse, stabbing chords are played:

on the beat ☐ off the beat ☑

8 The melody of this song moves:

mainly by step ☑ mainly by wide leap ☐

9 A suitable tempo marking for the music would be:

Adagio ☐ Moderato ☑ Presto ☐

CHAPTER 6 Music with a drone

Students' book: pages 48–53

Summary of students' material

different kinds of drone:
  single note – sustained or persistently repeated
  two (or three) notes – sounded together, or separately

drones changing in pitch

rhythmic drone

accompanying drone in Indian music

raga

discordant, concordant

Composer	Music	Genre/form/style	Culture/country of origin
CD 1.15 Anonymous	*Danse royale*	13th-century court dance	France
CD 1.16 Malcolm Arnold	Overture *Tam o'Shanter*	concert overture	England
CD 1.17 Haydn	last movement of Symphony No. 82 in C ('The Bear')	symphony	Austria
CD 1.18 ———	*Dingo*	didjeridu piece	Aboriginal traditional
CD 1.19 Somasundram Yasotha	*Sitar Ecstasy*	piece based on Kalyan raga	India
CD 1.20 S. Yasotha	*Bombay at Night*	pop disco piece	India

Page 49 **Answers** (Listening)

(*Danse royale*) Drone 1 matches the drone heard in *Danse royale*.

(Haydn) The grace notes sounding a semitone below the main drone notes. Also, the interval of a 5th in bars 22–25.

Page 50 **Using *Notate***

1 A sample student's piece, adding a drone bass to the tune at the top of page 50 of the students' book, is printed on pages 48 and 49 of this Resource Book. The music was edited by adding repeat signs and an extra two bars at the end. Voices selected:

Track 1 Trumpet
Track 2 StringLib-Soft
Track 3 StringLib-Soft

Tempo: ♩ = 110

2 Two sample settings of *Good King Wenceslas* with drone are printed on pages 50 and 51. Voices selected:

(a) Track 1 StringLib-Soft
Track 2 StringLib-Hard
Track 3 StringLib-Hard

Tempo: ♩ = 100

(b) Track 1 Clarinet
Track 2 StringLib-Soft
Track 3 StringLib-Soft
Track 4 Tambourine

Tempo: ♩ = 100

3 'Using a drone (2)' on page 52 of the *Notate* handbook could provide a further or alternative Composing activity.

Page 50 Further background notes on the didjeridu

- The didjeridu is played by male aborigines only – all boys are taught to play it from an early age.
- It is used – together with clapping sticks – to accompany singing and dancing, and also for 'open' (non-secret) ceremonies.
- The more-or-less conical tube is typically 1 to 1.5 metres long – though for some ceremonies, larger didjeridus are used which are 2.5 metres or more in length.
- The player may attack and release the drone note with soft or hard tongue technique, using single, double, or triple tonguing.
- Intervals used above the drone for hummed or sung notes are usually the 5th, octave, 9th and, especially, major 10th. Notes which are croaked or gurgled are often an augmented 11th (octave + augmented 4th) above the drone.
- Geographical area covered by the didjeridu: northern Australia.

Page 50 Answers (Listening)

1 The didjeridu player includes: varying the timbres by changing the shape of the mouth cavity, grunts, imitations of the dingo, tapping the tube with a stick.

2 The rhythm not included is rhythm (c).

Page 52 Background notes on *Sitar Ecstasy*, from north India

- The musical culture of the Indian subcontinent is one of the oldest and most revered in the world. There are two main musical traditions: Hindustani, of north India (including also Pakistan and Bangladesh); and Carnatic, of south India (south of Hyderabad).
- Almost all Indian classical music consists of three main elements:

  melody – often highly decorated with (microtonal) ornaments and nuances of pitch;

  a rhythmic accompaniment;

  an ever-present drone.

- The music consists mainly, sometimes entirely, of improvisation, and is based upon a chosen raga.

- A raga is an array of pitches – of melodic materials – which may be used to create a particular composition. Each raga has:

  an ascending form and a descending form (which may differ – as in Kalyan raga);

  characteristic ornaments and grace notes, and turns of melodic phrase;

  an association with a particular mood (*rasa*);

  a certain time of day or night when it should properly be performed, e.g. dawn, noon, evening, after sunset, midnight (Kalyan raga is properly performed 'during the first quarter of the night').

- The sitar is one of the most important instruments of India, especially in the north. It is a long-necked lute – the hollow neck being made of wood, and the body made of half a hollow gourd. There may also be an upper gourd. The sitar has sixteen to twenty-four curved, movable frets made of metal. There are seven metal strings, plucked with a wire plectrum worn on the forefinger. Five of these strings are melody strings, and the remaining two are drone strings. Running under the main strings there is also a set of a dozen or more sympathetic strings which give a characteristic shimmer to the tone. Among notable players of the sitar are Ravi Shankar, Ustād Vilayat Khan and, his son, Shujaat Khan.

- The tamburā is another type of long-necked lute, without frets. It supplies the accompanying drone. There are four metal strings, of which two are usually tuned to the upper tonic, one to the lower tonic, and one to the 4th, 5th, or 7th. The strings are strummed slowly and gently, one after another, with the forefinger, and are always played as open strings, never stopped.

- In Indian music, the seven degrees (*svara*) of the scale are called by these syllables:

  sa, ri, ga, ma, pa, dha, ni, (sa).

  Sa can be pitched at any level, to suit the voice or instrument of the main performer. Accompanying musicians tune their instruments to the chosen pitch.

Page 52 **Answers** (Listening)

The music becomes faster, more urgent and exciting, with a 'busier', more complicated texture.

Yes; towards the end there is a return to the opening pace and mood.

Page 53 **Answers** (Listening)

In *Bombay at Night* the Western instruments are: saxophone, electric guitar, (electric) bass guitar, and drum kit.

In *Within You, Without You* the drone is played on tamburā.

Page 53 Linked listening – recordings on cassettes

Item	Cassette
Indian raga	'Investigating Musical Styles', cassette 3 item 93
Neidhart von Reuental: *Winder wie ist nu dein Kraft*	'Enjoying Early Music'
Tchaikovsky: *Farandole* from Act 2 of *The Sleeping Beauty*	'Adventures in Music: Ballet'
Prokofiev: third movement from *Classical Symphony*	'Discovering Music' Book 1; 'Form and Design', cassette 2

Drone tune

20
1
2
3
25
1
2
3

Good King Wenceslas with drone (a)

Good King Wenceslas with drone (b)

CHAPTER 7 Chords and chord patterns

Students' book: pages 56–65

Summary of students' material

chord, triad
root, 3rd, 5th
tonic chord (I), dominant chord (V), and subdominant chord (IV)
doubling
chord-symbols
dominant 7th
using chord facility on electronic keyboard
12-bar blues pattern/progression
chorus
tonic seventh
muted brass
different kinds of chord-symbol (chart)
harmonic rhythm
blues notes
orchestration
repetition of chord pattern; bringing in new harmonies
chord guide (chart)
cadences
spacing

Composer	Music	Genre/form/style	Culture/country of origin
———	*My Lord, What a Morning*	spiritual	Afro-American
CD 1.21 Duke Ellington	*Black and Tan Fantasy*	12-bar blues	USA
CD 1.22 ———	12-bar blues pattern, played twice	———	———
CD 1.23 ———	12-bar blues pattern, played five times	———	———
CD 1.24 Tchaikovsky	'The Three Ivans' from *The Sleeping Beauty*	ballet	Russia

Page 56 Background notes on the spiritual *My Lord, What a Morning*

- The term 'spiritual' most often refers to religious folk-songs of black Americans, originating in the 19th century. They are mainly associated with the Afro-American church congregations of the American deep south.
- Some melodies are modal, and some use the pentatonic scale. Harmonies are similar to those of the 19th-century hymns. The rhythms are likely to be syncopated.
- Many spirituals make use of call-and-response patterns with solo singer answered by a group.
- Spirituals were brought to a wide audience beginning in 1871 when the Jubilee Singers of Fiske University (Nashville, Tennessee) toured the USA and then Europe, awakening interest in the genre as a concert item.
- The spiritual was one of the many ingredients which eventually blended together to become jazz.
- *My Lord, What a Morning* is particularly associated with the contralto, Marian Anderson. She often sang it in concert, and used the same title for her autobiography. She was the first black soloist to sing opera at the Metropolitan Opera House (New York), 7 January 1955, paving the way for many others. Marian Anderson died in April 1993, aged 94.
- Other well-known spirituals include: *Swing Low, Sweet Chariot, Sometimes I Feel Like a Motherless Chile, Steal Away, Nobody Knows the Trouble I See, Go Down, Moses*, and *Deep River*. (The last four of these were included by Tippett in his oratorio *A Child of our Time*.)

Page 57 A simple harmonization of *My Lord, What a Morning*, with words, and alto line added in the verse, is printed on page 55 of this Resource Book.

Page 60 The bass part played in the 12-bar blues pattern recorded on the CD is printed on page 55 of this Resource Book.

Page 61 Answer (Listening)

Harmonies different from the original chord pattern occur in playings 5 and 6, 9 and 10, 13 and 14, 15 and 16 – a rich change, beginning with supertonic 7th chord (F♯ maj7).

Page 63 Examples of rather more 'surprising' interrupted cadences:

Page 63 Answers

(a) perfect

(b) imperfect

(c) interrupted

(d) perfect

(e) plagal

Page 64 Using *Notate*

Composing idea No. 3: the chord progressions can be written on *Notate*, then played back (at a suitable tempo) as a background to the improvising of a melodic line. Adding a repeat sign *and* D.C. at the end will cause all the music up to that point to be played *four* times in succession. For example:

Page 65 Linked listening – recordings on cassettes

Item	Cassette
Handel: *Sarabande* from Keyboard Suite No. 11 in D minor	'History of Music', cassette 1
Jelly Roll Morton: *Dead Man Blues*	'New Assignments and Practice Scores', cassette 1 item 25
Louis Armstrong: *West End Blues*	'Investigating Musical Styles', cassette 1 item 39

My Lord, What a Morning

Bass part of the 12-bar blues

Listening Assignment D

Answers

Minuet in D from *Music for the Royal Fireworks* by Handel

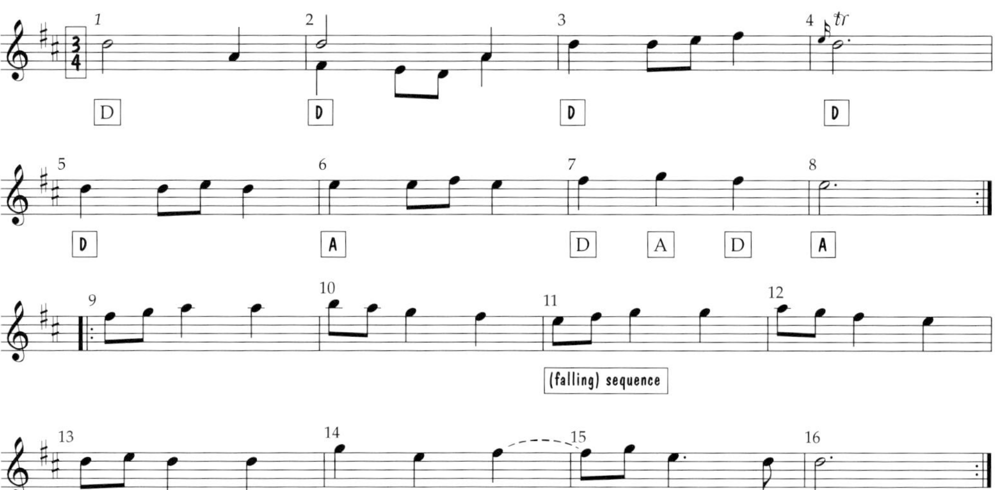

1 In the box after the key signature, write the correct time signature.

2 Add the missing notes in the empty bars 6 and 7.

3 Explain the meaning of :‖ at the end of bar 8 and the end of bar 16.

end of bar 8: repeat from the beginning
end of bar 16: repeat from bar 9/repeat from ‖:

4 The key of this music is D major. Bars 1 to 8 use only two chords:

chord I (tonic chord) = chord of D

chord V (dominant chord) = chord of A

In the boxes below bars 1 to 8, fill in the missing symbols. Four of them have already been done for you.

5 The music of bars 9 and 10 is repeated in bars 11 and 12 at a lower pitch. Write the name for this musical device in the box below bar 11.

6 A suitable dynamic marking for this Minuet would be:

f / forte

CHAPTER 8 Graphic notation

Students' book: pages 66–69

Summary of students' material

notation

various ways in which sounds may be notated

graphic notation

explanatory key; verbal instructions

turning graphics into sounds

creating graphics for sounds

graphic score (with key and explanation) to be interpreted

	Composer	Music	Genre/form/style	Culture/country of origin
CD 1.25	——	riff, on bass guitar, played three times	riff from a rock piece	——
CD 1.26–1.28	——	three sound-patterns, which students will create graphics for	——	——

Page 66 Answer (Listening)

Graphic C matches the bass guitar riff.

Pages 66/67 The six boxes of coloured graphics

Graphic notation is always, at least in detail, open to personal response and interpretation. However, some pointers:

Pitch (relative pitch) of the graphics is suggested in terms of relative height within each box.

Duration (imprecise, but relative) is suggested by length/width and horizontal placing and spacing, left to right, within each box. Silence is implied by any noticeable gap/space between graphics, moving from left to right.

That certain sounds should be smoothly joined together is indicated by continuing lines (boxes 5 and 6) or curving lines (boxes 1 and 2). That sounds should be disconnected from each other is implied by space between them, left to right, and short width (e.g. 'dots').

Contrasting or changing dynamics. In box 6, the expanding then contracting green triangular graphics might imply *crescendo* then *diminuendo*. In box 3, the two orange graphics might imply chords or clusters which expand in notes and/or volume – perhaps the first from ***mp*** to ***mf***, the second from ***mp*** to ***f***. Perhaps more arbitrarily, relative boldness/brightness of the colours might imply contrasting dynamics – e.g. in box 2: the green graphic perhaps ***mp*** or ***mf***, and red star perhaps ***f*** or ***ff***.

Pages 68/69

Several examples of graphic scores can be found in Chapter 9 of Reginald Smith Brindle's 'The New Music' (Oxford University Press, 1975).

CHAPTER 9 Ternary form

Students' book: pages 70–75

Summary of students' material

outline of ternary form
repetition, contrast
contrast between music A and music B
ways of making musical contrasts (chart)
unity, balance, variety
rhythmic feature
coda

Composer	Music	Genre/form/style	Culture/country of origin
———	Romanian folk-tune	folk-tune	Romania
CD 1.29 ———	*The Girls So Fair*	folk-dance in ternary form	Romania
Tchaikovsky	*Dance of the Flutes* from *The Nutcracker*	ballet; dance in ternary form	Russia
CD 1.30 George Enescu	*Romanian Rhapsody No. 1*	rhapsody for orchestra, based on folk-tunes	Romania

Pages 72/73 **Answers** (Listening)

First listening

1 The middle section (B) begins at bar 43.

2 Music A returns as A^2 at bar 62.

Second listening

1 Cor anglais

2 Ostinato

3 Tchaikovsky changes music A by making it much shorter – using bars 27–42 only.

Third listening

1 Tune A: wide range; some wide leaps; articulation more varied – staccato, legato (slurs), accents; note-values (durations) more varied than in Tune B.

Tune B: narrower range; movement by step, and in continuous semiquavers.

2 Contrasts between music A and music B include:

Music A	*Music B*
key: D major	key: F♯ minor
graceful, serene, delicate	forceful, rather agitated
light in texture	heavier, thicker in texture
above a pizzicato bass	all above a rhythmic ostinato
timbres: 3 flutes + strings, bassoon, cor anglais, and bass clarinet (mainly)	timbres: brass (trumpets, horns, trombones, tuba) + kettle drums and cymbals; then + strings and (low) woodwind
	a wider dynamic range: overall, louder – with many < >
	generally, lower in pitch than music A

Page 74 Sonia Delaunay's painting, 'Rythme Syncopé, dit Le Serpent Noir'

Repetition:
of colours – red, dark blue, light blue, blue-green, orange, yellow, grey, black and white; and of shapes – semicircles, squares, triangles and rectangles.

Contrast:
of colours of varying tones and intensities;
and of lines – straight lines and curved lines; and shapes – semicircles, squares, triangles and rectangles.

Page 75 Linked listening

The recitative *E pur così*, and aria *Piangerò*, from Handel's opera *Giulio Cesare* (Julius Caesar) typify two of the major conventions of opera and oratorio.

Recitative is a declamatory style of vocal writing in which the voice – half singing, half reciting – rises and falls according to the meaning of the text and closely follows the natural speech-rhythms of the words. Recitative is used especially in opera and oratorio as a means of swiftly carrying forward the plot – whereas an *aria* (Italian for 'song') is often reflective, tending to hold up the story.

By the end of the 17th century, two main types of recitative had developed. In the first type, called *recitativo secco* ('dry' recitative), the voice is accompanied only by continuo instruments – for example, the rhythmically flexible vocal line may be punctuated by chords on a harpsichord, with a cello strengthening the bass-line. The recitative *E pur così* is of this type. The second type, called *recitativo accompagnato* ('accompanied' recitative) or *recitativo stromentato* ('instrumented' recitative), may be used when the composer feels that the emotional or dramatic nature of the words needs heightening by a simple accompaniment for orchestra or at least for instruments besides those of the continuo group. Good examples of both these types of recitative can be found in numbers 14–16 of Handel's *Messiah*. No. 14 (*There were shepherds*) begins *secco*; then (at *And lo!*) becomes *stromentato*. No. 15 (*And the Angel said*) is *secco*. No. 16 (*And suddenly there was with the Angel*) is *stromentato*.

The aria *Piangerò* from *Giulio Cesare* is a typical *da capo aria* – that is, in ternary form (A^1 B A^2) but with only the first two sections written out. At the end of the contrasting section (B) the composer writes *da capo* (or simply *D.C.*) meaning 'from the beginning'. When repeating the opening section, the singer would be expected to add his or her own vocal ornaments and decorations to the printed melody. (Check whether this does, or does not, happen in your recording.) It also became customary to improvise a *cadenza*, a florid passage displaying the brilliance of the singer's technique, just before the final cadence of either B or A^2.

A translation of the text of this recitative and aria from *Giulio Cesare* together with musical examples and some background notes on this *opera seria* (a 'serious opera' in three acts) are given on page 7 of 'Musical Forms' Book 3 (Longman).

Page 75 Linked listening – recordings on cassettes

Item	Cassette
Prokofiev: *Masks* from *Romeo and Juliet*	'Musical Forms: Listening Scores'
Leroy Andersen: *The Typewriter*	'Adventures in Music ' Book 1

Listening Assignment E

Answers

Norwegian Dance No. 2 by Grieg

Grieg structures this dance in three sections of music.

First section

1 The tune is played by an oboe. Which of these shapes matches the opening notes of the tune?

(a) 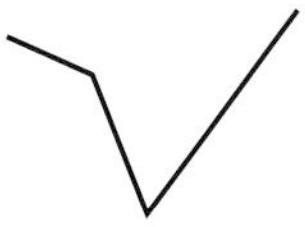 ☐ (b) 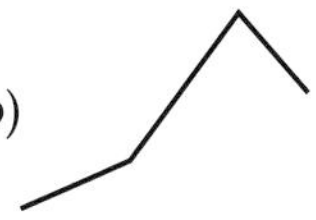 ☐ (c) 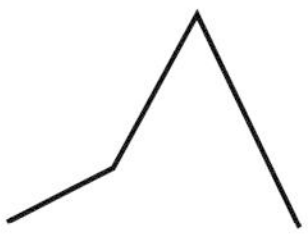 ✓

2 How are the string instruments being played to produce this kind of sound?

plucked/played *pizzicato*

3 The tune is immediately repeated. How are the violins played now?

with the bow/*arco*

Second section

4 The music of this section is:

(a) louder ✓ quieter ☐ and (b) slower ☐ faster ✓

5 The texture of the music is:

richer, denser than before ✓ clearer, thinner than before ☐

6 How does this second section end?

The music suddenly breaks off, followed by a pause (silence)

Third section

7 Does this section use the same tune as the first section, or does it use a completely new tune?

the same tune as the first section

8 The music of this Norwegian Dance is:

in $\frac{2}{4}$ time ✓ in $\frac{3}{4}$ time ☐

9 The music is structured in:

binary form ☐ ternary form ✓ rondo form ☐

CHAPTER 10 Using ostinatos

Students' book: pages 78–85

Summary of students' material

explanation of ostinato
kinds of ostinato (chart)
kwela
turning visual patterns into ostinatos
ground bass/basso ostinato
unity, variety
ground bass patterns
riff

Composer	Music	Genre/form/style	Culture/country of origin
CD 1.31 Anonymous	*Welscher Tanz*	Renaissance dance	Germany
Holst	*The Dargason* from *St Paul's Suite* (compared with the last movement – same music – of Suite No. 2 in F)	suite (for strings/ for military band)	England
Bizet	*Carillon* from *L'Arlésienne* Suite No. 1	incidental music to a play	France
CD 1.32 Sam Sklair	*Street Corner Kwela*	*kwela* (style of urban popular music)	southern Africa
CD 1.33 ———	*Induna Indaba* (Gathering of chiefs)	descriptive piece; Chopi xylophone orchestra	Mozambique
CD 1.34 Monteverdi	*Lamento della ninfa* (Lament of the nymph)	ground bass	Italy
CD 1.35 Graham Collier	———	riff, solo fills	England
CD 1.36 Haggett/Hodges	*Chance*	rock song	England

Page 78 **Answer** (Performing and Listening)

Rhythmic pattern 2 is repeated.

Pages 78/79 The last movement, *Dargason*, from Holst's *St Paul's Suite* is recorded on 'Instruments of the Orchestra', cassette 2. *Carillon* from Bizet's *L'Arlésienne* Suite No. 1 is recorded on 'Form and Design', cassette 2.

Page 78 **Answers** (Listening)

1 Holst varies the dynamics.

2 *Greensleeves*

3 The string section

Page 79 Background notes on *kwela*

- The Zulu word *kwela*, given to this style of urban popular music of southern Africa, is associated with 'social emancipation and increased intensity of life'. The word means 'go up and win' or 'attempt with success'. In the 1950s, *kwela* was performed on penny whistles by bands of young boys in the streets of the townships.
- The craze for penny whistle playing followed the screening of the African film 'The Magic Garden' in which music was played on penny whistle by a cripple boy.
- Later, the usual *kwela* ensemble included one or more flutes, one or two acoustic guitars, and a one-string bass.
- In Johannesburg, *kwela* is also called 'jive', and more recently has involved electrically-amplified instruments.

Page 79 Using *Notate*

(a) 'Using an ostinato' (1) and (2) on page 53 of the *Notate* handbook could provide extensions to the Composing activity. In (1), the ostinato might change at some point – then later return to the opening (given) pattern.

(b) An ostinato (or a ground bass – students' book page 81, Composing) can easily be set up on *Notate*, using the Copy facility. Page 70 of this Resource Book could be photocopied and handed out to students for them to follow the instructions.

Page 80 Background notes on *Induna Indaba*, from Mozambique

- The Chopi people of southern Mozambique, famous for their xylophone orchestras, are a small, isolated group of about 250,000.
- Instruments of the area include many varieties of xylophone, lamellaphone ('thumb piano'), rattle and shaker; also wind and string instruments; but drums are less frequently used.
- The usual Chopi orchestra includes about a dozen xylophones. These are of five sizes, covering a range of four octaves. The four-note double-bass xylophones provide a low rhythmic ostinato. The double-bass xylophones are played standing; the other sizes are played seated.
- All the xylophone bars are made of sneezewood. Below each bar is a resonator made from the shell of a wild orange, and each resonator has a buzzing membrane attached to it, over a small hole in its side.

- The Chopi xylophone orchestra is closely associated with *mgodo*, which is an orchestral dance form. In performances of *mgodo*, dance and music are synchronized by visual and aural cues between the leaders of the orchestra and the dancers.
- The music is based on a heptatonic scale, with the seven notes equally spaced. The texture of the music is polyphonic. Characteristic intervals: 4ths and 5ths
- There is often alternation between the tonic chord and the chord on the note immediately above.
- The orchestral dance form *mgodo* is a source of pride to the Chopi people and also to Mozambique as a whole.

Page 81 **Answers** (Jazz riff)

1 Trumpet and trombone

2 Nine times (in groups of three)

3 Answering solos (solo fills) are played in turn by: trombone, guitar, trumpet.

Page 83 **Answers** (with a suggested mark scheme for assessment)

Introduction tranquil, peaceful, calm, serene, haunting *(2 marks)*

Verse 1 drums *(1 mark)*

or: side/snare drum, bass drum, tomtoms, tenor drum *(4 marks)*

Chorus (3) some of the notes are different, some are the same as the vocalist's *(2 marks)*

Interlude 1 cymbals *(2 marks)*

Verse 2 three (C, D and E) *(4 marks)*

Chorus After the opening D minor chord, the harmonies change as follows:

[X] (Dm)
'Chance

X (C)
Look at the two of us e-vol-ving

X (Am) X (Dm)
Sil-hou-ettes of ro-mance hide from their eyes

Chance
X (C)
One of the two of us hides e-mo-tion

X (Am) X (Dm)
Me to you be-hind the scar of a lie.' *(6 marks)*

Interlude 2 acoustic (Spanish) guitar *(2 marks)*

Verse 3 This verse is shorter than the previous two, and is set to a different tune. *(4 marks)*

Coda 1 six times *(2 marks)*

2 After two playings of the new pattern, the first pattern returns. *(2 marks)*

(Total: 30 marks)

Pages 82/83 Background notes on the recording of *Chance*

The recording makes use of **sampling**. This is the recording of a single audio signal into a digital electronic memory. The note can then be replayed at different pitches via the keys on an electronic keyboard.

Sampling is a bit like recording the sound onto tape. Playing the tape faster will make the pitch of the sound higher. Playing it slower will make the pitch lower. Altering the speed will also alter the length of the playback:

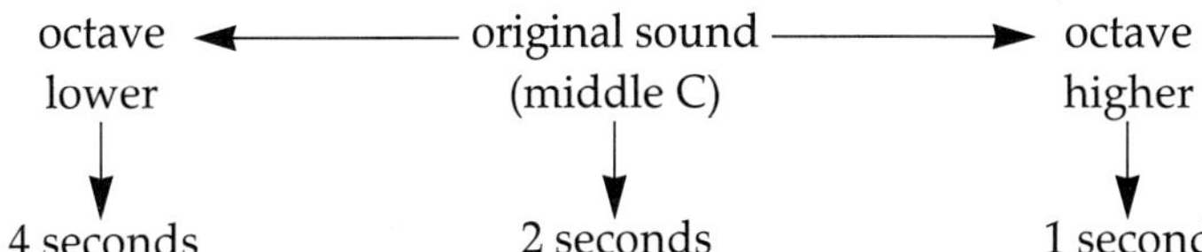

Since the sound is placed in an electronic digital memory, it can be saved to floppy disc, altered in the same ways that synthesizers work (ADSR – attack, decay, sustain, release – resonance, modulation, tuning, etc.) or taken into a computer and played with!

The flute sample in *Chance* was a 1-second sample of a single flute note (the note A above middle C). Once transferred to an electronic keyboard, it can be played as on any keyboard instrument. The knack is to play it with the inflections a flute player would use – rather than a keyboard player. And this holds good for any instrument that has been sampled.

Samplers are widely used for sampling voices and dialogue, and the concept behind sampling has been mainly responsible for the design of sound generation architecture of modern synthesizers. Traditionally based on common waveforms such as sine wave, sawtooth, square and triangle, many synthesized sounds are now based on samples of instruments and other sounds – thus expanding the sound production capabilities.

The very *beginning* of a sound is crucial in creating the particular timbre and effect of the note. The initial 'chuff' of a flute note helps us considerably to recognize and identify the sound as that of a flute rather than any other instrument. And so, in sampling, the important part of any sound is its beginning. This period of the sound is called the *transient* period.

After the transient period, a sound produced by a flute is basically a sine wave. And so in synthesis, the initial 'strike' is a sample of a flute, which then gives way to a synthesized sine wave.

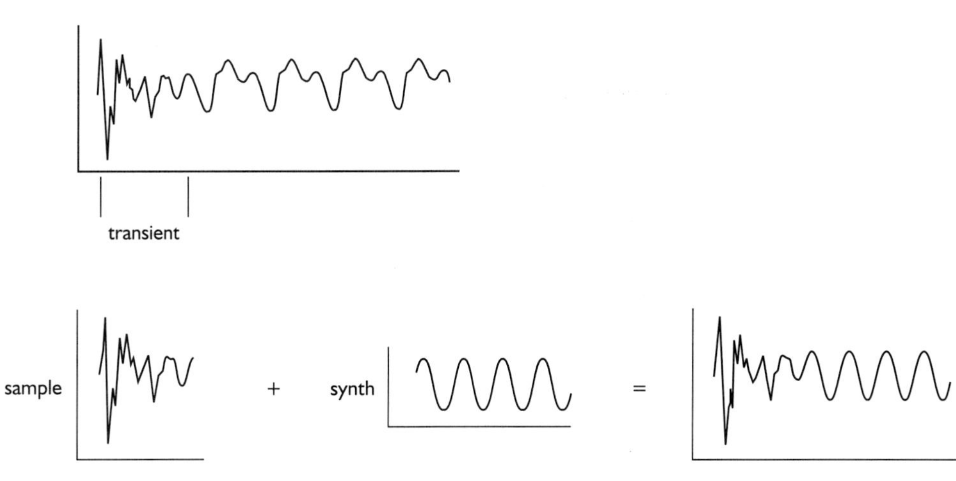

The 'voice length' is limited by memory. Therefore it is important to keep samples as short as possible. And so in this flute example, the sample consists of the transient period, plus one cycle of the sine wave. This cycle can then be *looped* to go on repeating until the key on the keyboard is released. 'Looped' means that this part of the sound is repeated or re-read from memory until released.

All the songs by the rock group Conquest were originally recorded on a **porta-studio**. This is a portable recording studio with four separate tracks available, so allowing one instrument to be recorded while listening to another previously recorded on another track – **multi-tracking**.

For example, if the drums were recorded on track 1, the tape would then be rewound and while track 1 was playing, the bass guitar would be recorded on track 2. Then while tracks 1 and 2 were played back, a rhythm guitar would be recorded on track 3.

The next step would be to 'bounce' (transfer) tracks 1, 2 and 3 onto track 4 – producing a mixed rhythm track of drums, bass and guitar.

Now tracks 1, 2 and 3 can be erased, allowing for the addition of keyboards, lead guitar, and vocals (both lead and backing).

The whole recording might happen like this:

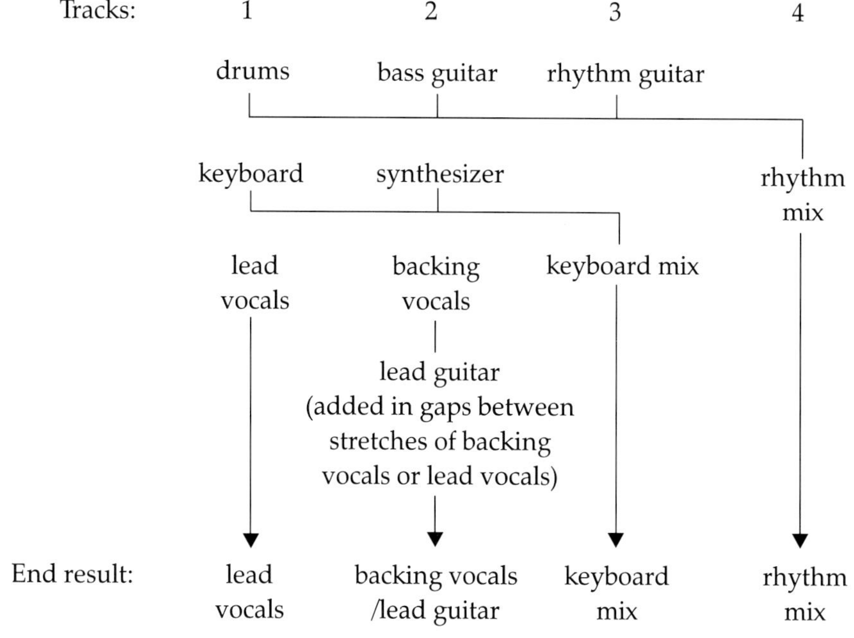

Although this arrangement would change with every song, it is possible to record up to ten instruments in this way if a source is added at each mix. For example:

	track	instruments
1 + 2 + 3 + source	= 4	4
1 + 2 + source	= 3	3
1 + source	= 2	2
source	= 1	1
		10 (total)

Later, ***Chance*** was re-recorded using more sophisticated IT equipment. This time, the group had at their disposal an 8-track studio with MIDI link via timecode, and a computer. (For MIDI and timecode, see pages 68 and 69.) This gave seven audio tracks, with track 8 being used for timecode and an infinite number of MIDI tracks.

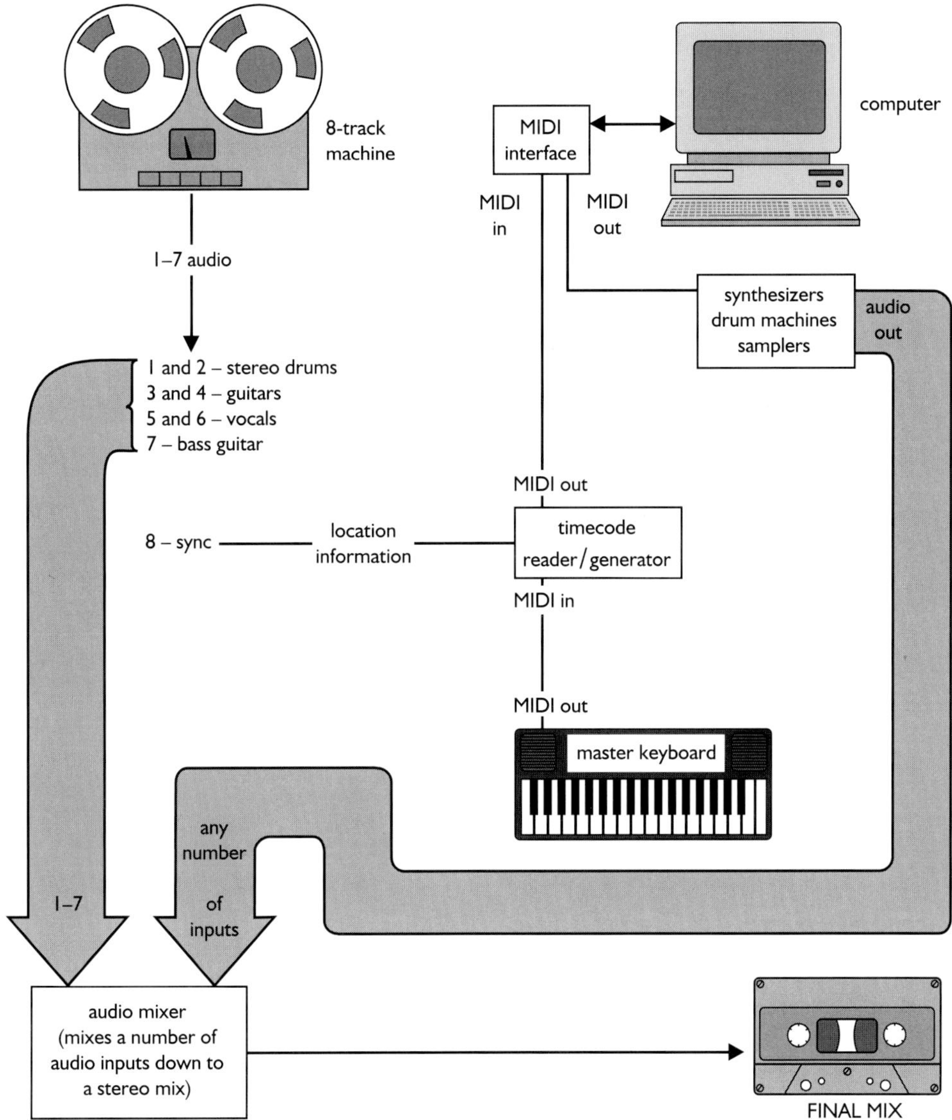

Method of recording

Structure of song assembled on computer – string synth + drum machine.
Computer synchronized to 8-track machine.
Drums recorded in sync with computer. (Drum machine then removed.)
Guide vocal recorded (eventually to be erased).
All guitars recorded.
Finished vocals recorded.
Bass guitar recorded.
Keyboard sounds (samples) and performances 'tweeked' (adjusted) to fit song.
All mixed down to DAT (Digital Audio Tape) with relative volumes of tracks adjusted.

The final mix used MIDI and computer facilities, and samples for IT. (It is this version of ***Chance*** which is recorded on the accompanying CD.)

MIDI (standing for Musical Instrument Digital Interface) is a computer-based language that allows suitably-equipped electronic instruments or devices to 'communicate' with each other. Possible MIDI instruments include:

- electronic keyboard/synthesizer
- drum machine
- sound sampler
- six-string electric guitar
- bass guitar
- electronic wind instruments (e.g. based upon saxophone, clarinet)

} if fitted with MIDI communications hardware

- MIDI sequencer

One 'controller' instrument can control a number of MIDI sound sources – which can be other MIDI instruments or just electronic boxes of stored sounds. Here, for example, are four linked electronic keyboards, each set to a different voice (timbre):

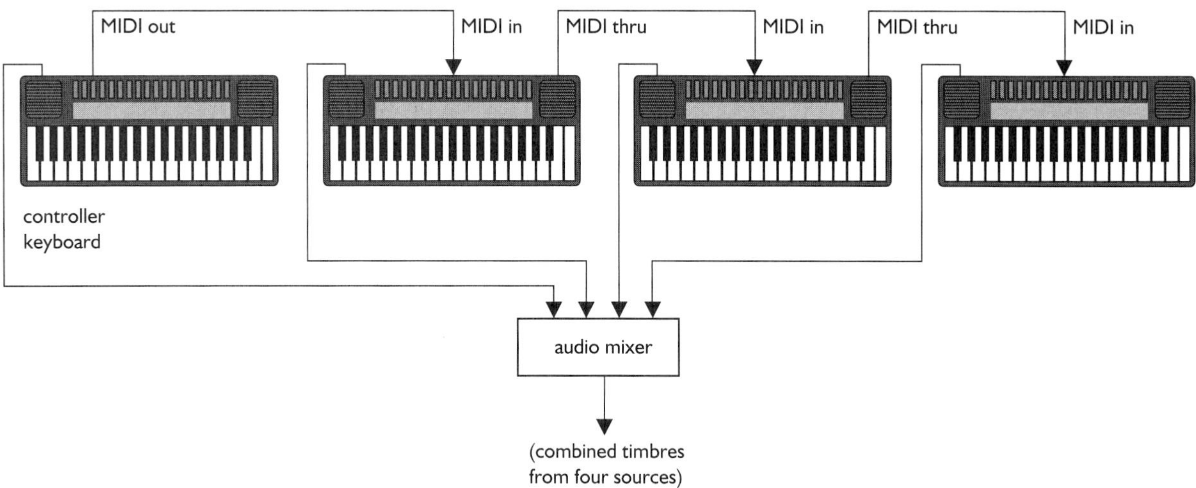

If, for instance, middle C is played on the controller keyboard, the note will sound from the controller and also, at the same time, from the other three keyboards – four different sounds (timbres) using the same note (pitch). In this way, a great variety of interesting blends of timbres can be created. A performance mode (e.g. pitch bend) on the controller will be instantaneously duplicated on the 'slaved' MIDI instruments.

MIDI language sends note information, and also note-on velocity (volume of note), note-off velocity (key release velocity at the end of the note), and after-touch – which allows velocity to be added after the note has been struck and then held for 'swell' (crescendo/diminuendo) effects. These are MIDI 'events'.

A MIDI **sequencer** adds the element of time to the above, allowing MIDI events to be recorded at a specific time, and acting as a digital language recorder – similar to a tape recorder in action but recording computer language rather than sounds.

When a MIDI sequencer recording is played back, the MIDI events are sent to responding MIDI instruments which generate the sounds. This allows the performance to be edited and refined, changing any sounds without re-recording the performance (as would be required with tape recording).

Timecode is an audio signal which tells a listening device any precise location on the audio tape. Such a device is a **timecode reader**. A generator is used to generate timecode in the first place. The timecode reader passes this information to a sequencer (in this case, the computer) via MIDI information, and the sequencer synchronizes with the tape. Move to another location on the tape, and the sequencer will follow. Play the tape, and the sequencer will play in sync – so enabling many MIDI compatible instruments to be added to the 'audio' recording.

Page 84 Composing/Improvising

The printout on pages 71 and 72 of this Resource Book, using *Notate*, shows the basic structure of the piece based on an ostinato and a riff. The voices selected in this case were:

Track 1 StringLib-Soft
Track 2 DrumKit1 (note C = BassDrum, A = CrashCymb)
Chords StringLib-Hard

Page 85 Linked listening – recording on cassettes

Item	Cassette
Purcell: *Dido's Lament*	'Form and Design', cassette 2
Walton: *The Death of Falstaff*	'Musical Forms: Listening Scores'
Chopin: *Berceuse* (extract)	'New Assignments and Practice Scores', cassette 1 item 39
Harrison Birtwistle: *Chronometer* (extract)	'History of Music', cassette 2

Using *Notate*

Repeating patterns

A repeating pattern such as an **ostinato** or **ground bass** can easily be set up on *Notate*, using the Copy facility:

- Notate the pattern once (as, for example, bars 1–4 below).
- Highlight the pattern as a grey block – move the mouse pointer to the left of the first note, press and hold down *select* and drag the pointer to the right until you include the last note. Click with *menu* and move the pointer to the word Edit. Pass right, highlighting the word Copy in black, and click with *select*. Move the insert pointer to the beginning of the first empty bar along the track and click with *select*. The pattern will be copied into the next bars. Click again with *select* to remove the highlight.

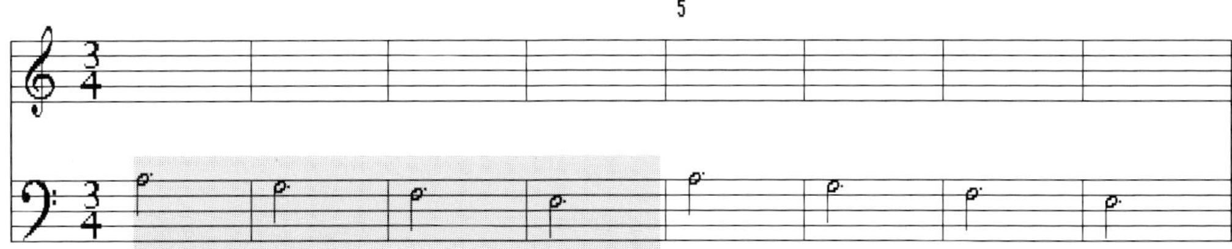

- To double the amount of music, highlight all the music written so far and copy, in the same way, into the next empty bar.
- A facility which may be useful is to insert a repeat sign (:‖) *and* D.C. as shown below. This will cause all the music up to that point to be played *four* times in succession.

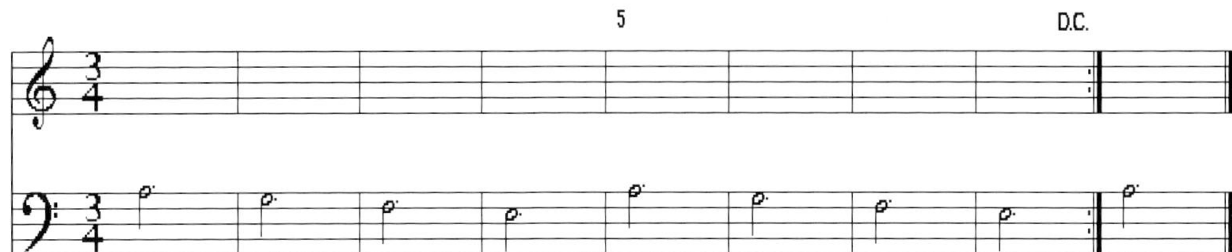

You could play back your repeating pattern on *Notate* and improvise against it, using voice or a suitable instrument.

RiffRap

(♩=120)
Am
Dm
Em
(repeat as often as necessary)
Am
(improvise, or rap)
Am
Dm
Em

Am
Am
Dm
Em
1
2

20
Am
1
2

CHAPTER 11 Some musical devices

Students' book: pages 86–93

Summary of students' material

decoration

ornaments (chart)

sequence – falling, rising

imitation – strict (an exact copy), free (a recognizably similar copy)

voice-exchange

Composer	Music	Genre/form/style	Culture/country of origin
CD 1.37 Chopin	Nocturne No. 2 in E♭	'character' piece for piano	Poland
———	*Es ist ein Schnitter* (He is a Reaper)	folk-melody	Germany
Brahms	Theme from *Variations on a Theme by Haydn*	melody based on sequences	Germany
CD 1.38 Bach	First movement from the Trio Sonata from *The Musical Offering*	trio sonata	Germany
CD 1.39 Anonymous, 13th century	*Alle, psallite cum luya* (*Alle* — praises sing with — *luya*)	motet, based on voice-exchange	England
CD 1.40 Traditional, arr. Henry Gheel	*Watching the Wheat*	arrangement of a folk-song	Wales

Page 86 Answer (Performing)

Another example of decoration occurs in bars 11/12.

Answer (Listening)

A^2 : bar 5 (beats 2 and 4) = decoration of bar 1;
bar 6 (first half) = decoration of bar 2;
bar 7 = decoration of bar 3 (trill, + extra G);
bar 8 = decoration of bar 4 (second beat, grace note added).

A^3 : bar 13 (first half) = further decoration of bar 1 (last beat, same as bar 5);
bars 14 and 15 decorate bars 2 and 3 in exactly the same way as bars 6 and 7;
bar 16 = decoration of bar 4.

Page 87

Examples of the ornaments on the chart may be found in the following music extracts printed in the students' book.
Chopin: Nocturne No. 2 in E♭ (page 86) – turn, upper mordent, trill, acciaccatura
Bach: *The Musical Offering* (page 89) – trill, appoggiatura
Bach: Two-Part Invention No. 1 in C (page 176) – upper mordent, lower mordent
Mozart: *Notturno* in D major (page 213) – acciaccatura, trill

Page 88 Answers (Performing)

1 Another sequence occurs in bars 9/10, 11/12, 13/14.

2 A falling sequence

3 Two bars

4 Two repetitions (three playings of the pattern in all)

Answers (Listening)

Sequences occur in:
(a) bars 2/3
(b) bars 7/8
(c) bars 11/12/13
(d) bars 15/16/17
(e) bars 20/21

They are:
(a) falling sequence, one repetition
(b) falling sequence, one repetition
(c) rising sequence, two repetitions
(d) falling sequence, two repetitions
(e) falling sequence, one repetition

Page 90 Answers (Listening)

1 Bars 9 and 11

2 Both have been heard earlier in the piece.

Pages 92/93 **Answers** (with a suggested mark scheme for assessment)

Introduction

The music is arranged for brass band. *(2 marks)*

Verse 1

(a) Bars 5/6 *(2 marks)*

(b) Bars 5/6 *(2 marks)*
and bars 13/14 *(2 marks)*

(c) Bars 9 to 12 *(3 marks)*

Bridge

Cymbal *(2 marks)*

Verse 2

(a) Bar 1 is decorated *(2 marks)*
and in bar 2, the last note is different (G instead of A). *(3 marks)*

(b) The rhythm ♫ is played, instead of ♪♬ *(3 marks)*

Bridge

Snare (side) drum *(3 marks)*
and cymbal. *(2 marks)*

A roll is played on the snare drum, *crescendo*, with a cymbal clash at the climax. *(4 marks)*

Verse 3

(a) Descant *(2 marks)*

(b) On the first beat of bars 9 and 10 *(4 marks)*

Coda

The brief Coda is simply an expressive repetition of the previous two bars. *(4 marks)*

(Total: 40 marks)

Page 93 Linked listening – recordings on cassette

Item	Cassette
Vivaldi: slow movement of *Winter* from *The Four Seasons*	'Form and Design', cassette 2
Mozart: slow movement of Clarinet Concerto	'Investigating Musical Styles', cassette 2 item 52
Stravinsky: *Sinfonia* from *Pulcinella*	'Enjoying Modern Music'
Anonymous: *Veris ad imperia*	'History of Music', cassette 1
Anonymous: *Sumer is icumen in*	'Enjoying Early Music'

CHAPTER 12 Mood and character

Students' book: pages 94–99

Summary of students' material

Music can immediately conjure up a mood

musical elements which may contribute to the mood or character (chart)

Japanese *gagaku* music (with example of notation)

changes and contrasts in mood and character

Composer	Music	Genre/form/style	Culture/country of origin
CD 2.1 Chabrier	*Marche joyeuse*	orchestral march	France
CD 2.2 Elgar	*Sospiri* (Sighs)	descriptive piece	England
CD 2.3 Berg	fifth movement from *Lulu* Suite	suite of pieces from an opera	Austria
CD 2.4 ———	*Etenraku* (Music coming through from Heaven)	court music for *gagaku* ensemble	Japan
CD 2.5 Tone Hulbaekmo	*Svevende Jord* (Floating Earth)	piece based on two contrasting moods	Norway

Page 94 Answers (Listening)

1 joyous, carefree (Chabrier: *Marche joyeuse*)

2 thoughtful, sad (Elgar: *Sospiri*, 'Sighs')

3 violent, menacing (Berg: Fifth piece from *Lulu* Suite – consisting of five pieces drawn from the opera *Lulu*. At this point in the opera, Lulu is being murdered by Jack the Ripper.)

1 (Chabrier)
rhythm – quick march rhythm, but varied (and sometimes unpredictable?)
tempo – brisk, lively
timbres – bright, scintillating, colourful (especially percussion)
based on major scale, in major key
intermittent effective use of silence

2 (Elgar)
tempo – slow
dynamics – fairly quiet
timbres – strings (lower strings muted), organ, harp (playing 'treading' chords)
melodic line – expressive, wide-curving, on (non-muted) violins
based on minor scale, in minor key (though modulating to relative major at end of extract)
effective use of silence after opening sustained chord

3 (Berg)
dynamics – mainly very loud
timbres – aggressive, especially brass, percussion (tam-tam, kettle drums, bass drum), high-pitched upper strings and woodwind
harmonies – harshly discordant

Pages 96/97 **Background notes on the Japanese *gagaku* piece, *Etenraku***

- The Japanese aesthetic approach to the arts is founded upon the philosophies of Shintō and Buddhism (especially Zen Buddhism).
- Japanese music has been influenced by the music of other cultures, such as China and Korea and, more recently, the West.
- *Gagaku* ('elegant music') is the traditional court music of Japan, played at ceremonies and banquets, and dating back to the Nara and Heian periods (8th to 12th centuries).
- The melody of the *shōkyoku* ('little piece') *Etenraku* is structured from the scale-type known as *ritsu*. When based on the note E, as here, it is called *hyōjō* ('E mode').
- Each melody instrument plays its own special version (in some cases, abstraction) of the *Etenraku* melody, resulting in a heterophonic texture.
- Characteristic elements: the importance of timbre, the slides and ornaments and microtonal bendings of pitches, the unhurried pace and free rhythm ('stretching' some beats).
- The members of a *gagaku* ensemble listen very carefully to each other. The rhythm is synchronized by correlating each part with the freely-moving main melodic line.
- The recording of *Etenraku* on the cassette is a shortened version – phrases A and B + *tomede* (coda). A full performance would include a third phrase, C, and follow the structure:

  || A | B | C | A | B | *tomede* ||

Page 96 **Answers** (Listening)

1 Dignified; solemn (austere); mysterious

2 The mood remains the same throughout

3 The timbres of the Japanese *gagaku* instruments; the tempo or pace – slow, unhurried, flexible ('elastic'); the melodic line and the intervals included and the ornaments – slides, nuances of pitch

Page 98 *Svevende Jord* (Floating Earth) is both composed and performed (using multi-tracking) by Tone Hulbaekmo.

Answers (Listening)

Section 1 is calm, peaceful, serene, haunting (sad)
Section 2 is carefree, joyous (happy)

Section 1: timbres (especially vocal tone), melodic lines, tempo/pace, harmonies
Section 2: metre, rhythm and accent (syncopation), tempo/pace, louder dynamic, timbres (especially percussion and vocal tone)

Page 98 Composing/Improvising

Students might notate their piece in the form of a graphic score, with explanatory key.

Page 99 Linked listening – recordings on cassettes

Item	**Cassette**
Copland: *Hoe-down* from *Rodeo*	'Adventures in Music: Ballet'
Shostakovich: *Polka* from *The Golden Age*	'Adventures in Music: Ballet'
Sousa: March – *Semper fidelis*	'Adventures in Music' Book 4

Listening Assignment F

Answers

Svevende Jord (Floating Earth), composed and performed by Tone Hulbaekmo

This music is structured in two contrasting sections.

First section

1 Arrange these in the order you hear them:

wooden flute   girl's voice   synthesizer

Write your answers in these boxes:

(a) synthesizer   (b) wooden flute   (c) girl's voice

2 The speed of this music is:

slow ☑   fast ☐   fairly fast ☐

3 The music of this section is:

always loud ☐   always quiet ☐

sometimes loud, sometimes quieter ☑

Second section

4 The music changes. Which two of these instruments do you hear?

violin ☑   wooden flute ☐   tambourine ☑   bass guitar ☐

5 When the singing begins, the synthesizer plays:

high-pitched notes ☐   low-pitched notes ☑

6 Compared with the music of the first section, this music is:

more rhythmic ☑   less rhythmic ☐

7 Just before the recording fades, the music:

slows down ☑   gets faster ☐

8 Which section of the piece do you like best? Why?

(personal response – expressing and justifying opinion/preference)

CHAPTER 13 Texture

Students' book: pages 102–107

Summary of students' material

types of musical texture

factors contributing to the texture

four basic styles of musical texture:
- monophonic/unison
- homophonic – melody (foreground) plus accompaniment (background)
- polyphonic/contrapuntal
- heterophonic

varying, contrasting textures

texture and timbre

changes in density of texture

Composer	Music	Genre/form/style	Culture/country of origin
CD 2.6 Ligeti	fourth movement from Chamber Concerto	chamber concerto for 13 players	Hungary
CD 2.7 Barber	*Adagio for String Orchestra*, Opus 11	piece for string orchestra	USA
CD 2.8 Stravinsky	*Sacrificial Dance* from *The Rite of Spring*	ballet	Russia
CD 2.9 Guillaume d'Amiens	*Prendés i garde* (Keep a good lookout)	medieval song in rondeau form	France
CD 2.10 Khatchaturian	slow movement from Piano Concerto	piano concerto	Armenia
CD 2.11 Bach	Contrapunctus 13 from *The Art of Fugue*	fugue	Germany
CD 2.12 ———	*Haunted Mountain*	folk-tune	Turkey
CD 2.13 Lutosławski	first movement from *Venetian Games*	orchestral work in four movements	Poland

Page 102 Answer (Listening)

1	Ligeti	light, open, thin, yet 'busy'
2	Barber	sustained, smooth, rich, flowing
3	Stravinsky	heavy, dense, thick, complicated

Page 103 Answers (Listening)

(*Prendés i garde*) The instruments taking part are: (sopranino) recorder and woodblock.

(Khatchaturian) Bass clarinet – at the bottom of the texture; piano – at the top of the texture.

Page 104 Background notes on *Haunted Mountain*, folk-tune from Turkey

- Due to the strong influence of radio and records, and school education in Western music, there has been some decline in the folk-music tradition of Turkey. However, folk groups are continually being founded to preserve and also breathe new life into the tradition.
- Whenever several musicians sing or play instruments together, they perform heterophonically.
- Turkish folk-music is based on a system of modes. *Haunted Mountain* is in a mode on A which includes the characteristic 'oriental effect' of an augmented 2nd.
- The rhythmic accompaniment to *Haunted Mountain* is played on *daff* (frame drum) and *darabukka* (single-headed goblet drum struck with both hands and used as an accompaniment to dancing).
- The *keman* (= European violin) has gained great popularity in professional folk-music in Turkey.

Page 105

The first movement of Lutosławski's *Venetian Games* contains certain aleatory ('chance-choice') elements. The notes are mostly printed in standard notation – but at times, players may choose their own speed at which to play them, and even choose from among the given notes the point at which to begin.

The movement is structured in eight sections, each of different duration. Lutosławski explains:

'The conductor gives the sign for the beginning and end of each section (the beat marking the end of section **A** also indicates the beginning of section **B**; the beat marking the end of **C**, the beginning of **D**; and so on). When the sign for the end of each section is given, performers must interrupt playing immediately. If before this time a player has already played his part to the end, he must start again from the beginning of that section. In sections **C**, **E** and **G**, the individual parts should not be played from the beginning but from any other point instead. Each player should play his part with the same freedom as if he were playing it alone. . .'

The following plan gives the approximate duration, and a brief description, of each of the eight sections.

A (12 seconds) For woodwind – but beginning with a sharp, incisive sound for percussion which in fact marks the beginning of every section.
B (26 seconds) For strings.
C (18 seconds) The music of **A**, now with kettle drums added.
D (about 22 seconds) For strings. The principal violinist, playing high harmonics, chooses at what pace to play his or her notes.
E (6 seconds) The music of **A** and **C**, now joined by music for brass.
F (2 seconds only) A single chord for strings.
G (24 seconds) The music of **A**, **C** and **E**, with piano duettists now joining in with bright, rhythmic splashes.
H (about 51 seconds) For strings, but ending with four spread-out sounds for percussion, the instruments dropping out one by one.

Changes in density of texture, and the effect of timbre and contrasts of timbre – main pointers:

- alternate sections (B, D, F, H) have a lighter, clearer, more open texture, and are for strings only – but exploit a variety of string timbres and colouristic effects, e.g. *col legno, harmonics, sul ponticello, tremolo sul ponticello, pizzicato;*
- the other sections (A, C, E, G) become progressively more dense in texture and varied in timbre by, at each stage, adding another instrument or group of instruments:
  woodwind only,
  woodwind + kettle drums,
  woodwind + kettle drums + brass,
  woodwind + kettle drums + brass + piano duet.

Page 106 Some students may care to create a piece which integrates two or more of the suggested textures in Composing ideas 1–4.

Page 106 Using *Notate*

The printout on page 84 of this Resource Book shows a sample student's piece in response to Composing idea No. 1. Voices selected:

Track 1 Flute
Track 2 Trombone (pitch tuned down one octave)
Track 3 Tambourine

Tempo: ♩ = 100

After some adjusting and editing, the piece was printed out and performed (on recorder, bass xylophone and tambourine) as one of a group of similar pieces at a school lunch-time concert.

Page 107 Linked listening – recordings on cassettes

Item	Cassette
Plainchant, medieval songs and dances	'Enjoying Early Music'; and 'History of Music' cassettes
Bizet: *Prélude to L'Arlésienne*	'Form and Design', cassette 2
Haydn: slow movement from *Trumpet Concerto*	'Enjoying Music' Book 1
Chopin: *Étude* No. 3 in E major	'Investigating Musical Styles', cassette 3 item 66
Bach: Fugue No. 9 from *The Art of Fugue* performed (a) by Philomusica of London, (b) by the Swingle Singers	'Investigating Musical Styles', cassette 2 items 46 and 47
Handel: *Hallelujah Chorus* from *Messiah*	'New Assignments and Practice Scores', Score 2

Chedington Fayre

Listening assignment G

Answers

First movement from *Venetian Games* by Lutosławski (Poland; 1913–1994)

(CD item 2.13)

Investigate the chart on sheet 2, which shows how this piece is built up. There are eight sections of music, each of different duration (section 6 is only two seconds long).

You will know when each section begins because, each time, there is a loud, explosive sound on percussion. The piece ends with four bars for percussion – the instruments dropping out one by one.

1 As you listen to the music:

(a) for each section, draw a wavy line in the top part of any box where instruments are playing (sections 1, 5 and 6 are already completed for you).

(b) under each wavy line you draw, write a dynamic marking – write:

f if the music is mainly loud,

p if the music is mainly quiet,

mf if the music is moderately loud.

2 When you have completed your chart, listen to the music again and answer these questions.

(a) Which section of the piece has the heaviest, most dense, most complicated texture?

Section 7

(b) Give the number of a section which has a light, thin, clear texture.

Section 2 or 8 (possibly 4)

(c) Each section begins with a loud sound played on four percussion instruments. Name one of them.

snare drum/tenor drum/claves/xylophone

(d) Which three of the following do you think are most important in creating the effect of the whole piece?

melody ☐ timbre ☑ texture ☑

dynamics ☑ rhythm ☐

(Continued on sheet 2)

Listening Assignment G

First movement from *Venetian Games* by Lutosławski (Poland; 1913–1994)

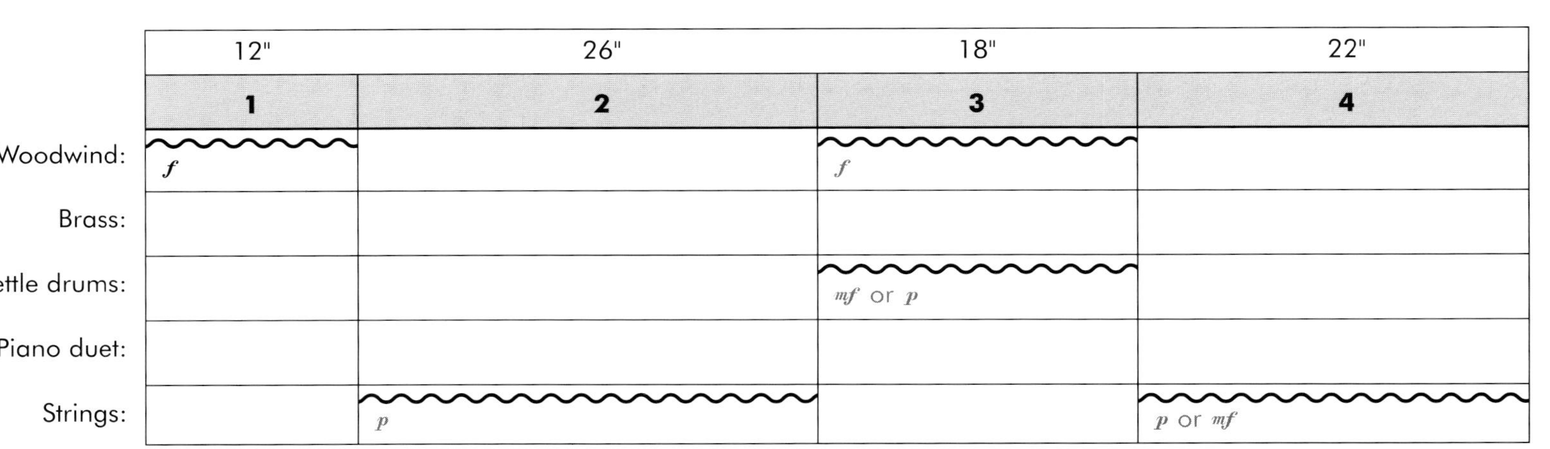

	12"	26"	18"	22"
	1	**2**	**3**	**4**
Woodwind:	~~~ *f*		~~~ *f*	
Brass:				
Kettle drums:			~~~ *mf* or *p*	
Piano duet:				
Strings:		~~~ *p*		~~~ *p* or *mf*

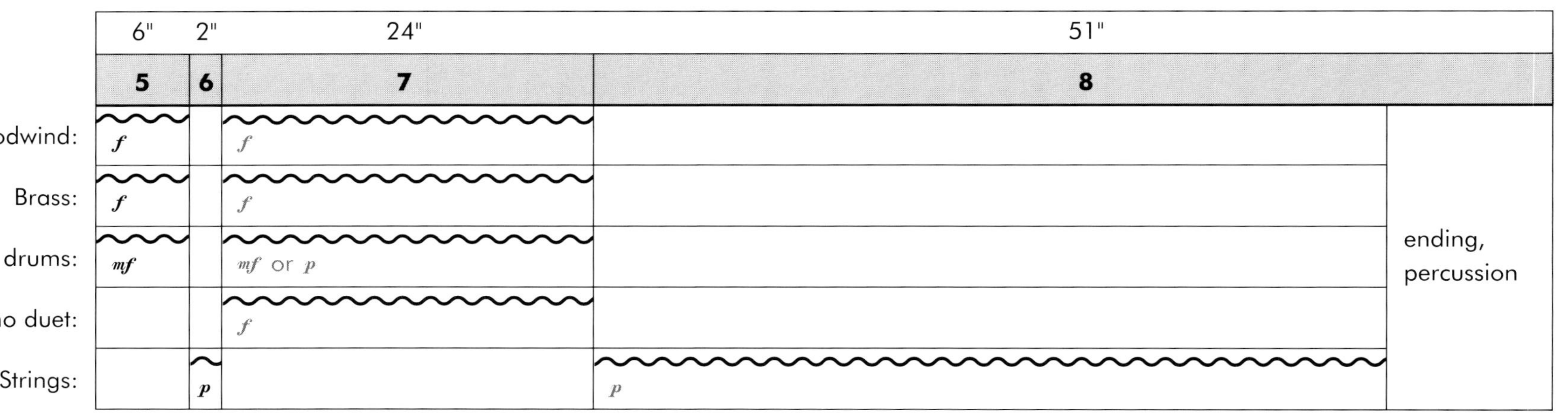

	6"	2"	24"	51"	
	5	**6**	**7**	**8**	
Woodwind:	~~~ *f*		~~~ *f*		ending, percussion
Brass:	~~~ *f*		~~~ *f*		
Kettle drums:	~~~ *mf*		~~~ *mf* or *p*		
Piano duet:			~~~ *f*		
Strings:		~ *p*		~~~ *p*	

CHAPTER 14 Rondo form

Students' book: pages 108–112

Summary of students' material

outline of rondo form
episode
link
coda
unity, balance
contrast, variety

Composer	Music	Genre/form/style	Culture/country of origin
———	*Seventeen Come Sunday*	folk-tune	England (Somerset)
CD 2.14 ———	*Folk-tune Rondo*	rondo form	———
CD 2.15 Järnefelt	*Praeludium* for orchestra	rondo form	Sweden
Purcell	Rondo from incidental music to *Abdelazar*	rondo form	England

Page 108 **Answer** (Listening)

The tune is played three times during the piece.

Page 110 **Answers** (with a suggested mark scheme for assessment)

1 Ostinato *(2 marks)*

2 Imitation *(2 marks)*

3 Any two of: key (A major, after F major); timbre (strings begin, after wind melodic lines in section A); texture; no ostinato; sustained chords; strings now *arco* (bowed) not *pizzicato*; drone bass (A, 7 bars, then D, 5 bars) *(4 marks)*

4 Drone *(2 marks)*

5 Oboe *(2 marks)*

6 Any three of: key and mode (D minor); rhythm; texture; tempo (slower); mood (reflective, wistful); dynamics (very quiet); timbre – quiet, expressive solos against ***pp*** rhythmic accompaniment *(6 marks)*

7 More wind instruments gradually join in; *(2 marks)*
repetitions of the pizzicato ostinato also have the effect of building up tension, excitement *(2 marks)*

8 The coda is based on the ostinato – at first, unison (4 bars), then singly, and rising in pitch: cellos, violas, second violins, first violins (their last two notes harmonized, tutti, as a perfect cadence) *(3 marks)*

(Total: 25 marks)

Page 111 Composing

Students might notate their rondo – either using conventional notation, or in the form of a graphic or diagrammatic score.

Page 111 Linked listening – recordings on cassettes

Item	Cassette
Couperin: Gavotte – *Les Moissoneurs*	'Form and Design', cassette 1
Purcell: Rondeau from *The Fairy Queen*	'Form and Design', cassette 1
Gluck: *Che farò senza Euridice*	'History of Music', cassette 2
Haydn: Finale from Piano Sonata No. 37	'Form and Design', cassette 1
Haydn: 'Gypsy' Rondo from Piano Trio No. 25 in G	'Discovering Music' Book 1
Mozart: Rondo from Horn Concerto No. 3	'Enjoying Music' Book 1
Bizet: *Prelude* to *Carmen*	'Adventures in Music' Book 2; 'Form and Design', cassette 2

Page 112 Answers

- The main rondo tune is heard three times.
- Purcell structures bars 3–6 of his main tune as a falling sequence.
- There are two episodes (B and C). B begins at bar 9. C begins at bar 25.

CHAPTER 15 Programme music

Students' book: pages 113–121

Summary of students' material

programme music, programmatic, programme
narrative, or descriptive
symphonic poem/tone poem
sections of the orchestra (in 'score order')
Dvořák's orchestra for *The Water Goblin*
typical layout of the orchestra
orchestral instruments (chart of drawings)
Chinese programmatic music
example of Chinese notation

	Composer	Music	Genre/form/style	Culture/country of origin
CD 2.16	Britten	*Storm* from *Peter Grimes*	operatic interlude	England
CD 2.17	Respighi	*The Villa Medici Fountain* from *The Pines of Rome*	symphonic poem	Italy
CD 2.18	Richard Strauss	The 'sheep episode' from *Don Quixote*	symphonic poem	Germany
CD 2.19–2.24	Dvořák	*The Water Goblin* (6 extracts)	symphonic poem	Bohemia (now Czech Republic)
CD 2.25	Kay Hua Heng	*Moonlight Night*	programmatic piece	China

Page 113 Answer (Listening)

1. a storm at sea
2. birdsong at sunset
3. a flock of sheep

Page 113 **Sample answers** (Listening)

1 A storm at sea (Britten: Fourth Sea Interlude, *Storm*, from *Peter Grimes*)
Ominous-sounding brass (trombones, then trumpets) with dissonant harmonies underpinned by rolls and thumps on bass drum (suggesting the violent movements of the water?); high, frantic violins against wild-sounding horns and aggressive rhythmic motives on kettle drums; a rising in pitch and increase in dynamic to *fff* (with high violins suggesting screaming gale-force wind?) and a crash on tam-tam at the climax (the crashing of a huge wave?)

2 Birdsong at sunset (Respighi: *The Villa Medici Fountain at Sunset* from *The Fountains of Rome*)
The hour of sunset evoked by calm, serene mood, hushed dynamics, fairly slow tempo/pace; birdsong suggested by melodic figures and especially trills on woodwind (clarinet, then flute, and later, piccolo), warm melodic figures on low violins; trills on other (muted) strings suggest rustling leaves; evening bells (celesta, glockenspiel)

3 A flock of sheep (Richard Strauss: *Don Quixote*)
Bleating and baaing sounds of a flock of sheep (realistically) suggested by major and minor 2nds on two oboes, against a *crescendo* on discordant muted brass (six horns, three trumpets, three trombones) and clarinets – all played with flutter-tonguing (the players roll the letter 'r' as they blow)

Page 114 The diagram shows the most often used layout – the aim being to achieve a balance and blend of the various instrumental timbres. The platform is usually terraced, with the loudest instruments placed highest, and furthest away from the conductor. The diagram also indicates the number of string players (here: 16 · 14 · 12 · 10 · 8) required in order to balance the sounds of woodwind and brass. Also, to balance sounds *within* the string section, the lower the pitch, the smaller the number of instruments needed.

Sometimes, the second violins are placed at the front on the right (with the cellos then more central) so that any antiphonal passages between first and second violins might be more clearly ('stereophonically') apparent – though the second violinists then have their instruments facing towards the back of the platform.

Some conductors have experimented with radically different layouts – notably Leopold Stokowski (six diagrams on page 688 of Volume 13 of 'The New Grove Dictionary of Music and Musicians').

Various examples of orchestral scores, of different genres and different periods, are included in 'Score-reading' and 'New Assignments and Practice Scores' in the Cambridge Assignments in Music series.

Pages 116/117 It might be profitable to discuss the 'dangers', in some cases, of being *too* literal in the interpretation of programme music. Also, consideration and discussion of the following:

- Could the piece function successfully without knowledge of the programme – i.e. as a piece of abstract music?
- Does knowing the programme (perhaps in some detail) enhance listening to the music?

Page 118 Background notes on the Chinese piece, *Moonlight Night*

- China's musical culture is one of the oldest in the world. It developed a musical system and musical instruments long before most other civilizations.
- Traditionally, Chinese instruments are classified into eight categories, according to their basic material: metal, stone, wood, clay, skin, bamboo, gourd, and silk.
- The two crucial elements in Chinese music are melody and timbre. The music is almost always in four-time, and the basic musical texture is heterophonic.
- Pentatonic scales are commonly used; but sometimes also a seven-note scale with five main notes and two auxiliary notes – as in *Moonlight Night*: main notes G A B D E, auxiliary notes F♯ and C.
- There are several types of Chinese musical notation, the earliest surviving type dating back to the 8th century. Most notations used by other Far Eastern cultures are adaptations or even copies of the Chinese systems.
- The *hsiao*, an end-blown flute, has seven finger-holes of which six are used to determine pitch. It is about 70 cm in length, with a range from d′ to around e‴. Its timbre is gentle and mellow, especially in the lower register, and its dynamic range is rather limited.
- The *erh-hu* is a two-string bowed lute. The hair of the bow is permanently caught between the two strings. The instrument is held vertically, with the resonator resting on the player's lap. One end of the resonator is covered with snakeskin. The *erh-hu* has always been popular in ensemble music, and the Peking opera, but during the 20th century it has also gained a reputation as a solo instrument.
- The *cheng*, a plucked half-tube zither, has a history dating back to the 9th century BC. It is the smallest of the three main Chinese zithers (the others are the *se* and the *ch'in*). The strings, usually sixteen in number, were formerly of silk, but are now more commonly of metal. They are plucked with the fingernails of the right hand. The left hand is used to press down on the strings, behind the bridges, to sharpen the pitches or add ornaments or vibrato effects. The sixteen strings are tuned to give three complete octaves of a pentatonic scale. Besides being used in ensemble music, the *cheng* has a large repertoire of solo pieces (all of them programmatic).

Page 118 Sample answer (Listening)

The music matches the title by being calm and peaceful in mood. The gentle, flowing movement and the zither's spread chords suggest clouds slowly drifting across the night sky, and the silvery timbre of the zither's high notes are like gleams of moonlight. The timbre of the low flute and erh-hu suggest that it's a warm night.

Page 119

The opening notes of *Chiang-hu-hsui* are:

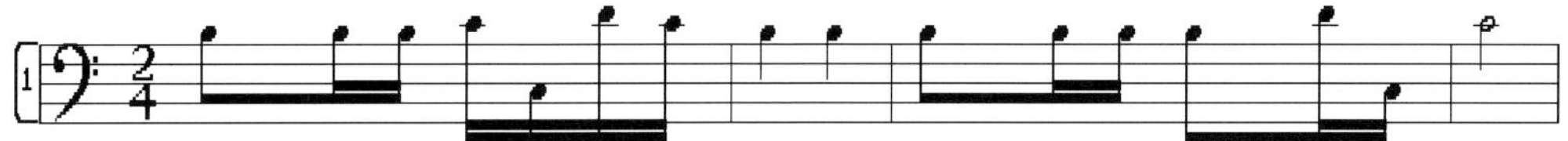

Page 121 Linked listening – recordings on cassettes

Item	Cassette
Smetana: *Vltava*	'Enjoying Music' Book 1
Saint-Saëns: *Danse macabre*	'Enjoying Music' Book 1
Musorgsky: *Night on the Bare Mountain*	'Enjoying Music' Book 1
Delius: *On Hearing the First Cuckoo in Spring*	'Musical Forms: Listening Scores'

Listening Assignment H

Answers

Listen to two pieces of programme music. Each paints a musical picture of the journey of a certain type of train:

A: *The Little Train of the Caipira* by Villa-Lobos

B: *Pacific 231* by Honegger

(A *caipira* is a Brazilian countryman. A locomotive of the 'Pacific' type would be used for heavy trains and high speed.)

In each of the following pairs of items, match one item to each piece. In the boxes, write:

A for the items which match *The Little Train of the Caipira*,

B for the items which match *Pacific 231*.

1 Low-pitched instruments (such as double basses) tell you when this train starts to move. B

Percussion instruments (such as various rattles and scrapers) tell you this train is starting to move. A

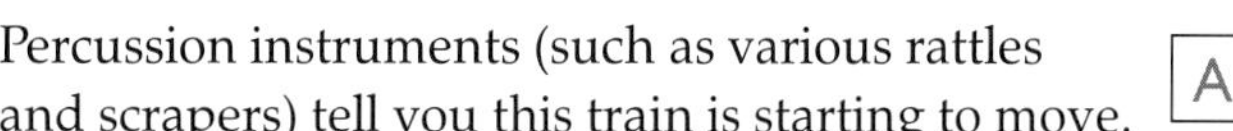

2

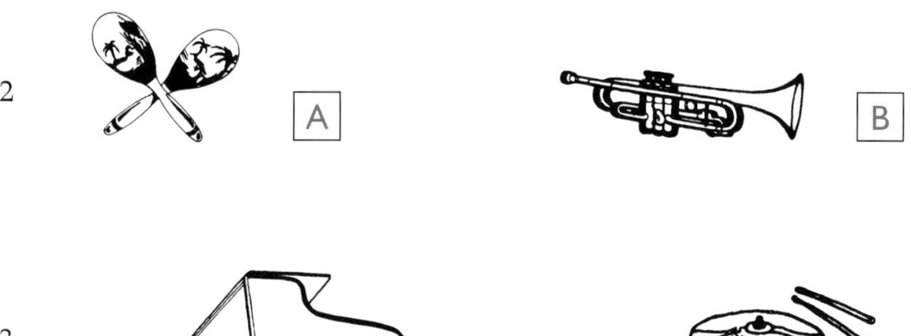

3

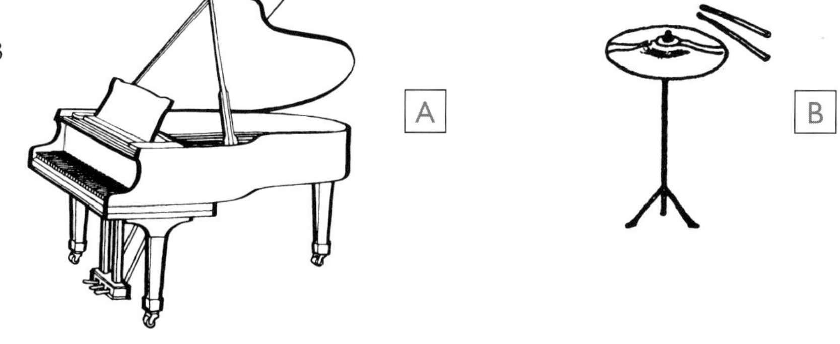

4

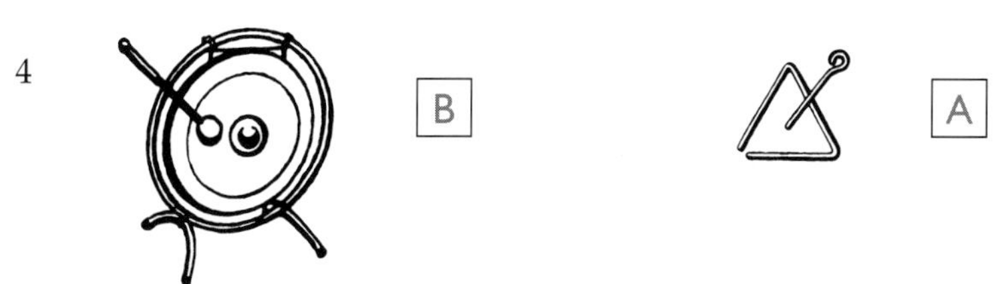

(Continued on sheet 2)

5 Rhythm of each main tune:

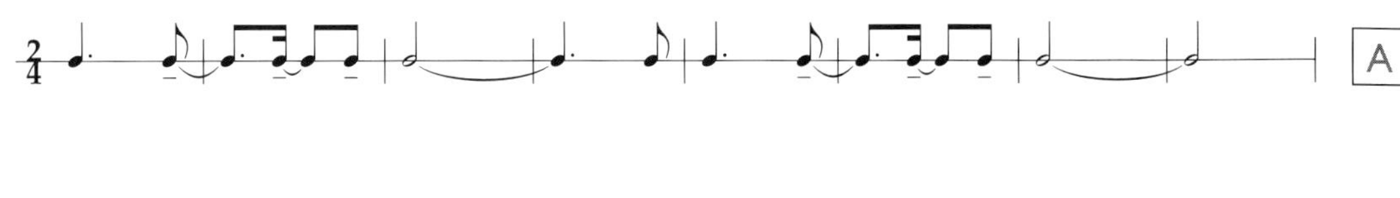

6 This train travels at more or less the same speed throughout its journey. B

During its journey, this train almost stops – but then picks up speed again. A

7 In this piece, the music ends as soon as the train has stopped. B

In this piece, the music continues for a while after the train has stopped. A

Which of these two pieces of programme music do you think is the most effective? In what ways?

(personal response – expressing and justifying opinion/preference)

CHAPTER 16 Timbre (2) – New sounds, new colours

Students' book: pages 124–131

Summary of students' material

timbre in 20th-century music

new sounds, new colours, new techniques:
- strings
- woodwind
- brass
- percussion

the 'prepared' piano

the 'string piano'

notations (chart)

Composer	Music	Genre/form/style	Culture/country of origin
CD 2.26 Penderecki	*Threnody: To the Victims of Hiroshima*	piece for string orchestra	Poland
CD 2.27 Berio	*Sequenza I*	piece exploiting solo flute	Italy
CD 2.28 Salzedo	*Interlude* from Divertimento	divertimento for three trumpets and three trombones	England
CD 2.29 Berio	*Sequenza V*	piece exploiting solo trombone	Italy
CD 2.30 Cage	*Second Construction*	piece for percussion ensemble	USA
CD 2.31 Cage	Interlude 2 from *Sonatas and Interludes*	piece for prepared piano	USA
CD 2.32 Vince Cross	*Night-Spell*	piece for 'string piano'	England

Page 124 Further details of Penderecki's *Threnody: To the Victims of Hiroshima*, together with some of his symbols and abbreviations and a page of the score (sections 26–37), are given on pages 56 and 57 of 'Enjoying Music' Book 3.

Page 125 A performance of Berio's *Sequenza V* for solo trombone includes certain elements of theatre. Details, together with information about a lengthier recorded extract of the piece, are given on page 246 of the students' book.

Pages 130/131 Linked listening – recordings on cassettes

Item	Cassette
Webern: No. 1 of *Five Movements for Strings*, Opus 5	'New Assignments and Practice Scores', cassette 2 item 6
Elisabeth Lutyens: opening of String Quartet No. 6	'New Assignments and Practice Scores', cassette 1 item 22
Birtwistle: *Verses for Ensembles* (first ten minutes)	'Investigating Musical Styles', cassette 1 item 41 B
Henze: Symphony No. 6 for two orchestras (last five minutes)	'Investigating Musical Styles', cassette 3 item 94
Varèse: *Ionisation*	'Enjoying Modern Music'
Cage: Sonata No. 2 (score printed in 'Enjoying Music' Book 3)	'History of Music', cassette 2
Cage: Interlude 1 (extract)	'Investigating Musical Styles', cassette 3 item 78
Cage: Sonata No. 5 (extract)	'New Assignments and Practice Scores', cassette 1 item 37
Tim Souster: *The Transistor Radio of St Narcissus* (two extracts) (for some background details about Tim Souster, see page 154)	'Investigating Musical Styles', cassette 3 items 88 and 89

CHAPTER 17 Words and music

Students' book: pages 132–139

Summary of students' material

mood, tempo, dynamics

types of voice (chart)

word-painting

hints on setting words to music

notating

sample varied texts for setting

words first, or music first, or 'words and music written hand in hand'

Composer	Music	Genre/form/style	Culture/country of origin
CD 3.1 Hamilton Harty	*Sea Wrack* (mezzo-soprano, piano)	song	Ireland
CD 3.2 Britten	*Midnight's Bell* from *Nocturne* (tenor, horn, string orchestra)	song-cycle for tenor, 7 solo instruments, and string orchestra	England
CD 3.3 Cross/Haggett/Hodges	*White*	rock song	England

Page 132 Moira O'Neill's poem, *'Sea Wrack'*

The mood of the poem is dark, melancholy, sombre – building to a mood of distraught grief, even despair.

The story which the poem tells, and also the characters which it portrays, are open to interpretation. The relationship between the two characters could be that of father and son, mother and son, or wife and husband (in some parts of Ireland a wife may refer to her husband as 'my lad').

The two characters earn a living by collecting sea wrack – the narrator managing their old brown boat, the second character cutting the wrack, which is later spread 'on the grey rocks to wither in the sun' and then burnt to kelp. The narrator falls asleep, and for some reason (unstated) the 'lad' sails the boat away from Cushendun. There is a full tide, and the swell causes the boat to sink; with no one within distance to help, he drowns.

Page 133 **Answers** (Listening)

1 The style of the accompaniment first changes at the line: 'The wet wrack'.

2 Harty takes as the climax the lines:

'There's a boat gone down upon the Moyle, an' sorra one to help!
Him beneath the salt sea, me upon the shore' …

3 A *crescendo* to *ff*, followed by a dramatic pause (silence).

Pages 136/137 For the possibility of more extended word-settings, lengthier versions of some of the suggested texts are printed as copymasters on pages 100–102.

Page 138 **Answers** (Listening)

1 Words in *White* which are in some way connected with water include:

(Rain) in my heart, tired (waters) collect,
(Spill) from my eyes the (streams) of regret,
The (rivers) of life (flow) through my veins,
My tortured body, my careless pain.

(White horses) of the (sea),
White horses carry me,
(Cascading) visions I see,
The (fountains) of life have betrayed me.

The shouts of emotion that no one can hear,
The poisoned orchid has flowered with fear,
A journey so long it may never end,
The wild (white waters) I've come to defend.

2 During the chorus, the three-chord progression is played four times.

3 In the interlude, the guitarist plays arpeggios.

Page 139 Linked listening – recordings on cassettes

Item	Cassette
Bennet: *All Creatures Now are Merry-minded*	'Investigating Musical Styles', cassette 1 item 33
Weelkes: *As Vesta Was from Latmos Hill Descending*	'History of Music', cassette 1
Vautor: *Sweet Suffolk Owl*	'History of Music', cassette 1
Purcell: *Dido's Lament*	'Form and Design', cassette 2
Schubert: *The Erlking*	'Discovering Music' Book 2
Schubert: *Death and the Maiden*	'Musical Forms: Listening Scores'
Britten: *Now the Great Bear and the Pleiades* from *Peter Grimes* (described in 'Musical Forms' Book 3)	'History of Music', cassette 2

Spring

Spring, the sweet spring, is the year's pleasant king;
Then blooms each thing, then maids dance in a ring,
Cold doth not sting, the pretty birds do sing:
  Cuckoo, jug-jug, pu-we, to-whitta-woo!

The palm and may make country houses gay,
Lambs frisk and play, the shepherds pipe all day,
And we hear ay birds tune this merry lay:
  Cuckoo, jug-jug, pu-we, to-whitta-woo!

The fields breathe sweet, the daisies kiss our feet,
Young lovers meet, old wives a-sunning sit,
In every street these tunes our ears do greet:
  Cuckoo, jug-jug, pu-we, to-whitta-woo!
    Spring! the sweet spring!

Thomas Nash

from The Way through the Woods

They shut the road through the woods
  Seventy years ago.
Weather and rain have undone it again,
  And now you would never know
There was once a road through the woods . . .

Yet, if you enter the woods
  Of a summer's evening late,
When the night-air cools on the trout-ring'd pools
  Where the otter whistles his mate
(They fear not men in the woods
  Because they see so few)
You will hear the beat of a horse's feet
  And the swish of a skirt in the dew,
  Steadily cantering through
The misty solitudes,
  As though they perfectly knew
The old lost road through the woods . . .
But there is no road through the woods.

Rudyard Kipling

Dream (*Sueño*)

My heart rests near the cool fountain.
  (Bind it with your threads,
  spider of oblivion.)
The water murmurs its song to my heart.
  (Bind it with your threads,
  spider of oblivion.)
My awakened heart tells of its loves.
  (Spider of silence,
  weave your mystery.)
The water of the fountain listens, sombrely.
  (Spider of silence,
  weave your mystery.)

Federico García Lorca

from The Forsaken Merman

Now the great winds shoreward blow;
Now the salt tides seaward flow;
Now the wild white horses play,
Champ and chafe and toss in the spray.
Children dear, let us away!
This way, this way!

Call her once before you go —
Call once yet!
In a voice that she will know:
'Margaret! Margaret!'
Children's voices should be dear
(Call once more) to a mother's ear;
Children's voices, wild with pain —
Surely she will come again!
Call her once and come away;
This way, this way!
'Mother dear, we cannot stay!
The wild white horses foam and fret.'
Margaret! Margaret!

Come, dear children, come away down;
Call no more!
One last look at the white-wall'd town,
And the little grey church on the windy shore,
Then come down!
She will not come though you call all day;
Come away, come away! . . .

Matthew Arnold

Jabberwocky

'Twas brillig, and the slithy toves
Did gyre and gimble in the wabe;
All mimsy were the borogoves,
And the mome raths outgrabe.

"Beware the Jabberwock, my son!
The jaws that bite, the claws that catch!
Beware the Jubjub bird, and shun
The frumious Bandersnatch!"

He took his vorpal sword in hand:
Long time the manxome foe he sought —
So rested he by a Tumtum tree,
And stood awhile in thought.

And as in uffish thought he stood,
The Jabberwock, with eyes of flame,
Came whiffling through the tulgey wood,
And burbled as it came!

One, two! One, two! And through and through
The vorpal blade went snicker-snack!
He left it dead, and with its head
He went galumphing back.

"And hast thou slain the Jabberwock?
Come to my arms, my beamish boy!
O frabjous day! Callooh! Callay!"
He chortled in his joy.

'Twas brillig, and the slithy toves
Did gyre and gimble in the wabe;
All mimsy were the borogoves,
And the mome raths outgrabe.

Lewis Carroll

CHAPTER 18 Making comparisons

Students' book: pages 140–143

Summary of students' material

comparing folk-tune settings by Balakirev and Tchaikovsky

comparing orchestrations by Ravel and Ashkenazy

comparing settings of the Dies irae

Composer	Music	Genre/form/style	Culture/country of origin
CD 3.4 Balakirev	*Overture on Three Russian Themes*	concert overture	Russia
CD 3.5 Tchaikovsky	Finale of Symphony No. 4 in F minor	symphony	Russia
CD 3.6 Musorgsky	*The Old Castle* from *Pictures at an Exhibition* orchestrated by Ravel	orchestration of a suite for piano	Russia/France
CD 3.7 Musorgsky	*The Old Castle*, orchestrated by Ashkenazy	orchestration of a suite for piano	Russia/Iceland
CD 3.8 Verdi	Dies irae from *Messa da Requiem*	Requiem	Italy
CD 3.9 Britten	Dies irae from *War Requiem*	Requiem	England

Page 140

Answers (Performing)

1 Four phrases

2 Three bars in each phrase

3 Minor

Answers (Listening)

1 Balakirev's music, in the first two playings of the tune, most closely matches the original.

2 Tchaikovsky inserts an extra two beats at the end of each phrase – actually making each phrase two bars of $\frac{4}{4}$. He repeats, exactly, the melody of phrase 1 and phrase 2, and of phrase 3 as phrase 4 (as, in fact, does Balakirev in his third presentation of the tune).

3 Instrumentation of the playings of the tune:

Balakirev
(i) clarinet
(ii) oboes – joined by bassoon in second half
(iii) upper strings – second violins and violas (pizzicato), with each note repeated, off the beat, by first violins (arco)

Tchaikovsky
(i) flutes, clarinets, bassoons
(ii) two horns
(iii) trombones, tuba, and double basses

4 Balakirev uses no percussion in this extract.
Tchaikovsky, in (iii), adds excitement by bringing in cymbals and triangle on the 'extra' two beats at the end of each phrase.

Page 141 **Answers** (Listening)

1 Both orchestrators give X to bassoon.
Ravel gives Y to alto saxophone; Ashkenazy gives Y to cor anglais.

2 Ravel: (muted) strings
Ashkenazy: harp, low wind, low strings

Page 142 **Answer** (Listening)

Both extracts are for four-part choir (SATB) and full orchestra. Britten first uses male voices only; then female voices (occasionally + tenors). Verdi only occasionally uses the sections of the choir separately – otherwise, SATB together.

Both composers make dramatic use of brass and drums (Britten alternates brass fanfare passages with choral/orchestral passages). Verdi also makes distinctive use of woodwind instruments, especially piccolo, to add brilliance.

Both composers exploit a wide dynamic range from ***pp*** to ***ff***. The Verdi extract begins ***ff***, then becomes quieter (***pp***, *sotto voce* in verse 2). Britten begins ***pp***, with < > (especially in the male voices passage), then varies the dynamics considerably.

The Verdi extract is in four beats to a bar throughout – frequently with an emphasis on (weak) beats 2 and 4; often there are rhythmic patterns of swift-repeated notes for the four trumpets. Britten alternates $\frac{4}{4}$ brass passages, often with the rhythm | ♪ ♩. 𝅗𝅥. | followed by a bar containing triplets, with $\frac{7}{4}$ choral/orchestral passages with the rhythm | ♩ 𝄽 ♩ 𝄽 ♩ ♩ 𝄽 |.

Towards the end of the Verdi extract, words are whispered/softly spoken. In the Britten extract, all the words are sung.

Page 142 Using *Notate*

The printout on pages 106–109 is of a student's piece in response to Composing idea No. 3. Voices selected:

Track 1 StringLib-Soft
Track 2 StringLib-Steel
Track 3 TomTom
Track 4 CrashCymb
Chords StringLib-Soft

Tempo: ♩= 110

Page 143 Linked listening

On 'Keyboard Instruments' cassette there are comparative extracts of:
Froberger: *Lament Composed in London* played (a) on harpischord, (b) on clavichord;
Bach: *Chromatic Fantasy* played (a) on Shudi and Broadwood harpsichord,
(b) on Steinway concert grand piano.

Russian Folk-tune

20
25
Em
Em
Em
Em
Em
1
2
3
4

30
Em
B7
B7
Em
1
2
3
4
B7
35
B7
Em
Em
Em
Em
40
Em
Em

Em
B7
B7
45
Em
B7
B7
Em
50

Listening Assignment I

Answers

Listen to two contrasted dances:

A: English Dance No. 4 by Malcolm Arnold

B: *Masks* from the ballet *Romeo and Juliet* by Prokofiev

In each of the eight musical categories below, match the descriptions to the dances. In the boxes, write:

A if the description matches English Dance No. 4, or

B if the description matches *Masks*.

(Use pencil – in case you have second thoughts!)

1	**Tempo:**	moderate speed	B	fairly fast	A
2	**Melody:**	medium in range, moving by step and narrow leap	A	wide in range, and including wide leaps	B
3	**Metre:**	3 beats to a bar	A	4 beats to a bar	B
4	**Rhythm:**	regular, steady	B	much use of syncopation	A
5	**Texture:**	mainly heavy, rich, dense	A	mainly light, clear, open	B
6	**Harmonies:**	mainly concords	B	spicy discords at times	A
7	**Dynamics:**	very loud (*ff*) almost throughout	A	varying over a wide range (*pp* to *ff*)	B
8	**Character:**	forceful, energetic, heavy-footed	A	carefree, jaunty, bouncy	B

Which of these two dances do you like best? Why?

(personal response – expressing and justifying opinion/preference)

CHAPTER 19 Rhythm (2)

Students' book: pages 146–155

Summary of students' material

binary form

$\frac{2}{4}$ time

$\frac{6}{8}$ time

simple time, compound time

time signatures, simple and compound (chart)

syncopation

ways of creating syncopation

irregular times/metres:

$\frac{5}{4}$ and $\frac{5}{8}$, $\frac{7}{4}$ and $\frac{7}{8}$, $\frac{11}{8}$

polyrhythm – 'rhythmic counterpoint'

Composer	Music	Genre/form/style	Culture/country of origin
CD 3.10 Mozart	last movement of Serenade No.12 in C minor (K388): Theme	serenade for wind octet	Austria
CD 3.11 Mozart	Variation 2, from the same	serenade for wind octet	Austria
——	*L'autre jour en voulant danser* (The other day as I was dancing)	folk; dance-song	France
CD 3.12 Mozart	last movement of Serenade No.12 in C minor: Variation 3	serenade for wind octet	Austria
Schumann	opening of Scherzo from Symphony No.4 in D minor	scherzo from a symphony	Germany
Tchaikovsky	*Dance of the Cygnets* from *Swan Lake*	ballet	Russia
Khatchaturian	*Waltz* from *Masquerade Suite*	orchestral suite	Armenia
Scott Joplin	*Maple Leaf Rag*	piano rag	USA
Tchaikovsky	opening of third movement of Piano Concerto No. 1 in B♭ minor	piano concerto	Russia
CD 3.13 ——	*Dangle Dance*	folk-dance	Romania
CD 3.14 ——	*Glare pu petas?* (Where are you flying to, seagull?)	folk-tune	Greece
CD 3.15 Branislav Kovacev	*South of the Border Dance*	dance in folk style	Bulgaria
CD 3.16 ——	Tahitian drum music	traditional drum-patterns	Polynesia
CD 3.17 Louis Armstrong	*Struttin' with Some Barbecue*	trad jazz	USA

Using *Notate*

Ideas in the *Notate* handbook which could link to this chapter include:
'Dividing the beat into 3' (page 48)
'Syncopation' (page 48)
'Using different rhythms together' (page 49)

('Syncopation' – this idea could be developed/extended by students by adding another 4 (8, 16) bars of syncopated rhythm patterns of their own.)

Page 147 **Answer** (Performing)

The melody of *L'autre jour en voulant danser* ends, unusually, on the supertonic (rather than on the tonic, or on a note of the tonic chord).

Page 149 *Maple Leaf Rag* by Scott Joplin is recorded on the cassette accompanying 'Adventures in Music: Ballet'.

Page 150 **Answer** (Listening)

Tchaikovsky includes these ways of creating syncopation:
(a) Placing an accent on a weak beat (e.g. bars 1–3, 5–16, and, especially, 29–36).
(b) Placing a rest on the strong, first beat of a bar (bars 21–28).
(c) Placing an accented chord between beats – off the beat, or on a subdivision of the beat (in bars 21–27, the accompanying strings play a chord on the first beat of each $\frac{3}{4}$ bar and another on the fourth quaver – i.e. *between* beats 2 and 3).

Pages 151/152 **Background notes**

1 *Dangle Dance*, folk-dance from Romania
- Most Romanian folk-songs and dances are linked with the various events of the human life cycle. The folk-music has been best preserved in the remote and isolated mountainous regions.
- In Romanian folk-song, the rhythm is based on the combination of two units of duration, one short and one long – either in the ratio of 1 : 2 or the ratio 2 : 1. In folk-dances, however, the ratio is quite likely to be 2 : 3 or 3 : 2 (as in *Dangle Dance*).
- Each region of Romania has its own distinctive types of folk-dance. Most of them are performed by large groups, dancing in a circle or semi-circle, or in single file (see students' book, page 70), or in couples.

2 *Glare pu petas?*, folk-tune from Greece
- Modern Greek folk-music can be classified according to three categories: folk-songs, folk-dances, and dance-songs or choral dances.
- There are at least seven distinct regional styles. Each has been influenced musically by neighbouring Balkan or eastern Mediterranean countries.
- A 7-beat metre ($\frac{7}{4}$ or $\frac{7}{8}$) is most characteristic.
- If danced, *Glare pu petas?* would be a *kalamatianos* – a chain dance structured in four-bar phrases in 7-beat metre, performed in an open circle. The leader dances improvised figures and athletic leaps while the other dancers repeat a basic step-pattern.
- The bouzouki firmly established itself as the leading instrument in urban popular music in Greece, and also among Greeks who have settled elsewhere.

3 *South of the Border Dance*, from Bulgaria

- Bulgaria has a particularly rich heritage of folk-music and folk instruments. Folk customs, accompanied by music, show historical connections with the cultures of the various peoples who inhabited the area long before the Slavs and Bulgarians arrived there.
- A great number of Bulgarian folk-songs and dances are in irregular metres, such as $\frac{5}{8}$ (or $\frac{5}{16}$), $\frac{7}{8}$, $\frac{11}{8}$, $\frac{13}{8}$.
- Melodies are diatonic, and usually narrow in range – the $\frac{11}{8}$ melody of *South of the Border Dance* typifies these points (range of only a 4th).
- This dance is a *khoro*, a round-dance. The basic movements would include leaps and hops, and steps on the whole foot, on the tip of the toe, on the heel.

Page 152 Answer (*South of the Border Dance*)

3 (c) The music changes to $\frac{3}{4}$ time (metre).

Page 152 Background notes on the drum music from Tahiti

- Drum ensembles are extremely popular, especially accompanying Tahitian dances such as the *'ōte'a*, a lively group dance. The accompaniment consists of 'rhythmic counterpoint' played on three to ten *tō'ere* (slit drums) of different sizes and pitches, one or more *tariparau* (double-headed barrel drum), and often a *tini* (five-gallon paraffin can).
- Another popular dance is the *hivenau*, a round-dance whose accompanying music consists of a call-and-response song originating from 18th-century European sea shanties which Tahitians would have heard sung by sailors of ships such as the *Bounty*.
- Other types of Tahitian music-making include polyphonic choral singing of traditional Tahitian texts, and *'utē* – songs with or without accompaniment by instruments (such as guitar and harmonica) and/or other voices.

Page 154 Answers (Listening)

3 (a) Banjo
(b) Chorus 2 – A: clarinet; B: trombone
Chorus 3 – trumpet
(c) The coda is a simple repeat of the previous two bars.

Page 155 Linked listening – recordings on cassettes

Item	Cassette
Gershwin: *I Got Plenty o' Nuttin'* from *Porgy and Bess*	'Adventures in Music: Opera'
Britten: *Old Joe Has Gone Fishing* from *Peter Grimes* (described in 'Musical Forms' Book 3)	'History of Music', cassette 2
Bernstein: Psalm 100 from *Chichester Psalms*	'Investigating Musical Styles', cassette 1 item 11
African polyrhythms	'Investigating Musical Styles', cassette 1 item 14
Stravinsky: *Procession of the Sage* from *The Rite of Spring*	'History of Music', cassette 2

CHAPTER 20 Chords and clusters

Students' book: pages 156–162

Summary of students' material

intervals

each interval has its own distinctive character or 'flavour'

consonance, dissonance

concords, discords

triads – major, minor

seventh chords – minor 7th, major 7th

ninth, eleventh and thirteenth chords

chromatic notes, chromatic chords

note-clusters/cluster chords

notations of note-clusters (chart)

suggested ways of using note-clusters

Composer	Music	Genre/form/style	Culture/country of origin
Grieg	*In My Native Country*	lyric piece for piano	Norway
———	*Black is the Colour of My True Love's Hair*	folk-tune	USA
———	*Ein Jäger aus Kurpfalz* (A hunter from Kurpfalz)	folk-tune	Germany
CD 3.18 Jim Northfield	*Accusations*	note-cluster piece for acoustic and electronic keyboards	England

Page 156 Answers

Most dissonant are minor 2nd and major 7th, followed by major 2nd and minor 7th.

Chord (3) has a minor 7th; chord (4) has a major 7th.

Page 157

Other possible versions are:

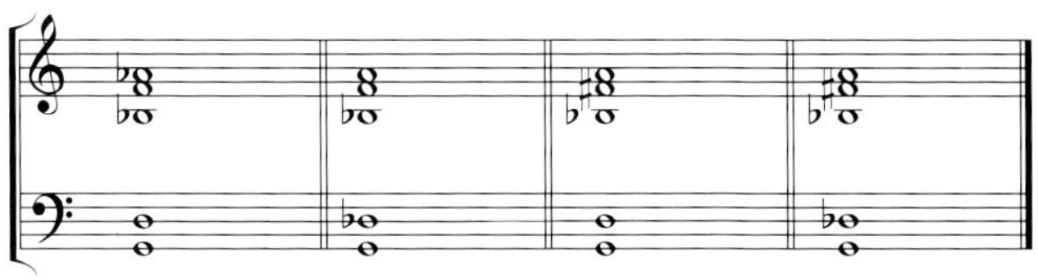

Page 157 The beginning of Grieg's *In My Native Country* (No. 3 of *Lyric Pieces* Book 3, Opus 43), showing seventh, ninth, and thirteenth chords:

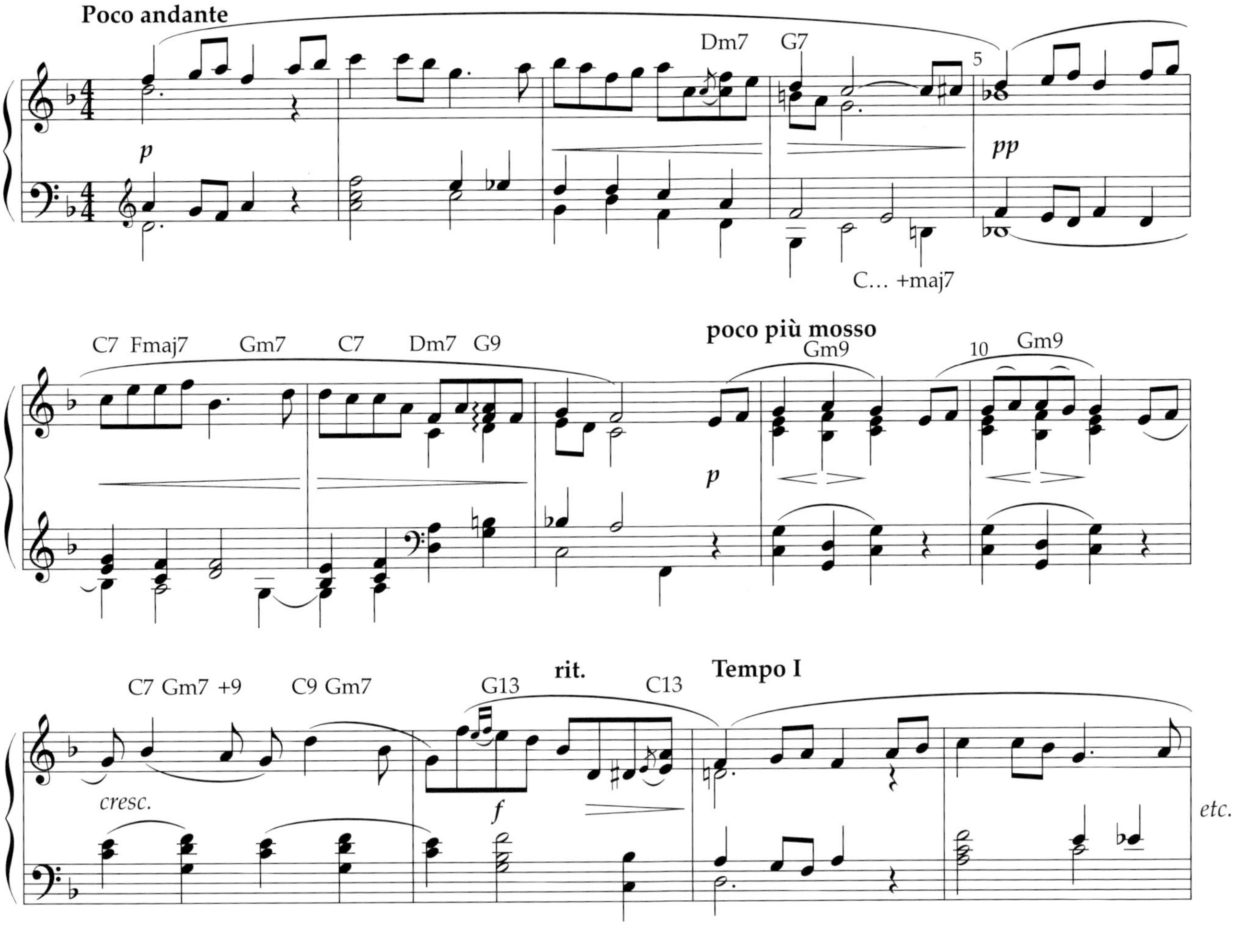

Poco andante
Dm7 G7
5
p
pp
C… +maj7
C7 Fmaj7 Gm7 C7 Dm7 G9
poco più mosso
Gm9
10 Gm9
p
C7 Gm7 +9 C9 Gm7
G13
rit.
C13
Tempo I
cresc.
f
etc.

Page 158 Using *Notate*

Chords can be added to *Black is the Colour* using *Notate* – but as the program can only add one chord per bar, the melody must first be edited by converting it into $\frac{2}{4}$ time. Instructions are given on page 116 of this Resource Book, which could be photocopied and handed out to students.

Page 117 shows the resulting printouts of the two harmonizations – the first using triads only, the second including seventh chords and one ninth chord.

Page 118 shows a sample keyboard arrangement, following the second chord scheme.

Page 158 Sample harmonization of *Ein Jäger aus Kurpfalz*:

F Am Dm7 Gm9 C C B♭maj7 C7
5
F F Am7 Dm7 Gm9 C C7 Gm9 C7 F
10
15

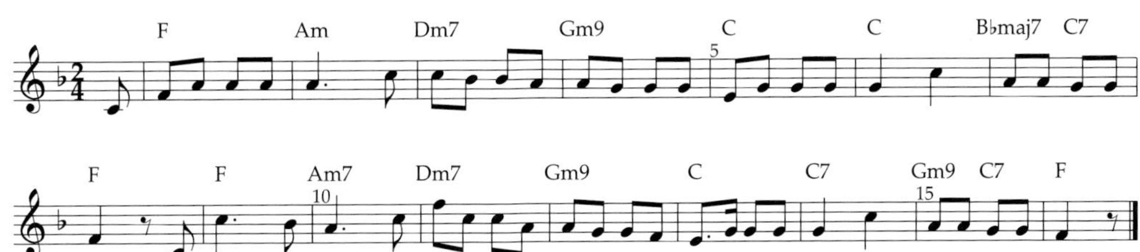

Page 158 Using *Notate*

Black is the Colour

You can add chords to the melody of *Black is the Colour* using *Notate*. However, as *Notate* can add only one chord to each bar, you must first edit the melody by converting it into $\frac{2}{4}$ time. It could, of course be written on *Notate* in $\frac{4}{4}$ time (copied from page 158), and then copied to another window with a $\frac{2}{4}$ time signature:

- Having notated the melody in $\frac{4}{4}$ time, open up another window. Hold down Ctrl on the keyboard and press F7. Change the time signature to $\frac{2}{4}$ and click on OK.
- Highlight the entire $\frac{4}{4}$ melody as a grey block.
- Move the mouse pointer to the $\frac{2}{4}$ window and click with *menu* to display the main menu. Move the pointer to Edit and pass right, highlighting the word Copy. Click with *select*. Move the insert pointer to the $\frac{2}{4}$ time signature and click with *select*. The melody will appear in $\frac{2}{4}$ with ties added where necessary. (Do not discard the $\frac{4}{4}$ version of the melody.)
- Now add chord symbols above the appropriate notes, according to the first chord scheme on page 158.
- Open another window, and make another copy of the $\frac{4}{4}$ melody, edited into $\frac{2}{4}$ time. Add chord symbols according to the second chord scheme on page 158. You will need to replace the Dm9 chord with Dmin7 – but as the 9th itself (note E) is in the melody, the musical effect will be the same.
- Play each of the $\frac{2}{4}$ harmonized versions. Which do you prefer, and why? (Select a tempo which matches the mood and character of the music – and also suitable voices for the melody and the chords.)

Black is the Colour

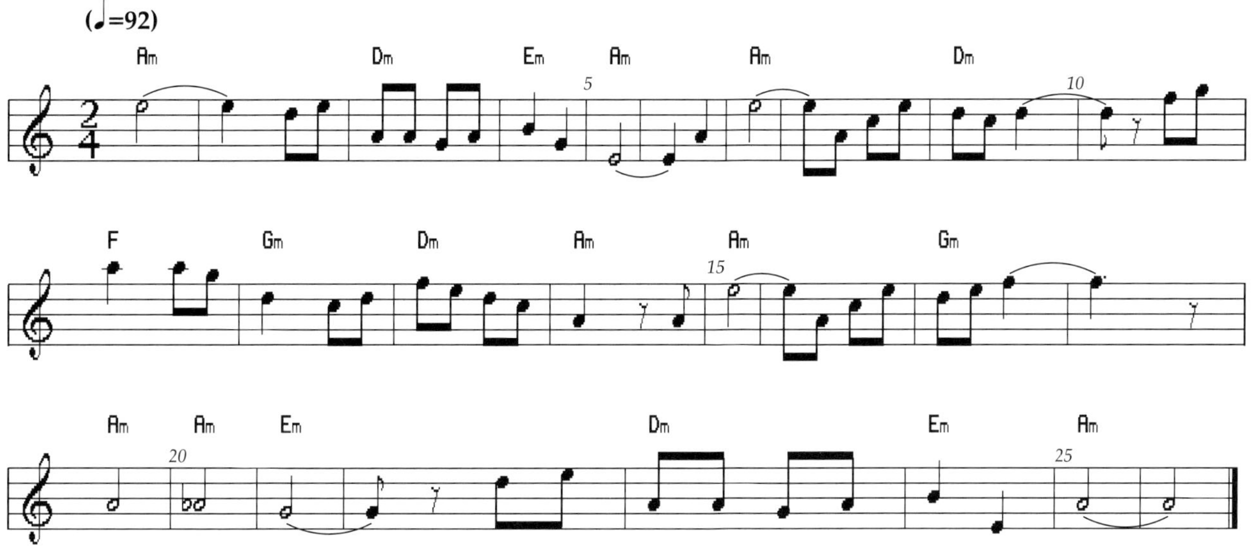

Black is the Colour

Black is the Colour

Listening Assignment J

Answers

The Devil's Dance from *The Soldier's Tale* by Stravinsky

A In this piece, you will hear the sounds of ten instruments. Look at this chart:

Woodwind	Brass	**Strings**	Percussion
clarinet	trumpet	violin	3 snare drums, with snares lifted
bassoon	trombone	double bass	bass drum

The names of some of the instruments are already filled in. And the name of one of the four sections of the orchestra.

Listen to *The Devil's Dance*, and fill in the missing words.

B Listen again to *The Devil's Dance*. For each of these five categories, tick the description which you think best matches the music.

(1) **Melodies:** long and flowing ☐ short and spiky ☑

(2) **Dynamics:** mainly quiet ☐ mainly loud ☑

(3) **Tempo:** quite fast ☑ fairly slow ☐

(4) **Rhythms:** energetic, syncopated ☑ smooth, relaxed ☐

(5) **Harmonies:** mainly concords ☐ mainly discords ☑

C Look at the group of instruments on the right. Name the instrument in the group which does *not* take part in *The Devil's Dance*.

cello

Name the instruments which take part in *The Devil's Dance* which are *missing* from the group.

clarinet, trumpet, double bass, bass drum

CHAPTER 21 Music as background to words

Students' book: pages 163–169

Summary of students' material

musical accompaniment or background to spoken words – recited in strict time, or spoken 'in free time'

alternation of music and text, perhaps with some overlapping – or a more continuous musical background (care in synchronization)

usually the music closely follows and reflects the mood and meaning of the text

Composer	Music	Genre/form/style	Culture/country of origin
CD 3.19 Walton	*Tango-Pasodoble* from *Façade*	poem spoken against background music	England
CD 3.20 Honegger	*The Incantation of the Witch of Endor* from *King David*	dramatic scene declaimed against background music	Switzerland

Pages 163/164

Edith Sitwell quickly earned a reputation as a controversial figure – eccentric even – theatrical in both dress and manner. At the time of *Façade*, Walton was sharing a house with the Sitwells, and so there was close and constant contact between poet and composer.

As Sitwell explained, her poems are abstract poems, patterns in sound – concerned more with the *sound* of words than their precise meanings. The poems were investigations into the effects of rhythm, speed (changes of speed are important in *Tango*), and, especially, patterns of rhyme.

Rhymes are placed at the end of lines, and also at different places in the line – for example:

'black cape', 'slack shape';
'trees', 'ease';
'Thetis', 'treatise', 'wheat is', 'cheat is'.

Certain 'key' rhymes are spaced out throughout the poem – for example:

'Pasquito', 'bandito', 'mosquito';
'hide tide', 'ride', 'bride', 'guide'.

Page 165 Listening

To tackle the Listening task, it could be suggested to students that they first list letters (a) to (k), then while listening to the two pieces write W (for Walton, piece 1) and/or H (for Honegger, piece 2) alongside the appropriate letters.

Answer

(a) H
(b) W
(c) W
(d) H
(e) W H
(f) H
(g) W
(h) H
(i) (neither)
(j) H
(k) W

Page 166 Composing

Students might notate their background music in the form of a graphic score, with an explanatory key.

Page 169 Linked listening

The Incantation Scene in the Wolf's Glen from Weber's *Der Freischütz*, described in detail in 'Musical Forms' Book 3, is recorded on 'History of Music', cassette 2.

CHAPTER 22 Tension – and release

Students' book: pages 172–175

Summary of students' material
tension achieved by a *combination* of musical elements and devices
ways of building up tension and excitement (chart)
ways in which tension may be released or relaxed (chart)

Composer	Music	Genre/form/style	Culture/country of origin
CD 3.21 Barber	*Adagio for String Orchestra*	piece for string orchestra	USA
CD 3.22 Prokofiev	opening of *Montagues and Capulets* from *Romeo and Juliet* Suite 2	orchestral suite from a ballet	Russia
CD 3.23 Musorgsky	'The scene with the chiming clock' from *Boris Godunov*	dramatic scene from an opera	Russia

Page 172 Teachers may prefer first to ask students to give opinions on how tension/release can be achieved (perhaps using one or more of the examples mentioned on page 175) *before* investigating the material in the boxes on pages 172 and 173.

Page 173 **Answer** (*Adagio for String Orchestra*)

Barber releases the tension with a dramatic pause (silence), followed by very much quieter music at a lower pitch (darker, richer, mellower, less strident sounds).

Pages 173/174 **Sample answers**

1 Prokofiev: *Montagues and Capulets*
Tension built up by: roll on cymbal and discord built up on brass in a *crescendo* from ***mf*** to ***ff***, woodwind and other percussion joining in, ***ff***, at bar 3. Released by silence from woodwind, brass and percussion at the end of bar 4, to reveal a concord (chord of B minor) on muted strings – playing, ***ppp***, since bar 3, but unheard till now.
The process is repeated (though this time, the strings are playing a chord of Amaj7).

2 Musorgsky: 'The scene with the chiming clock'
First build-up of tension (Boris feels he is suffocating – sometimes sings, sometimes speaks anguishedly): the ticking of the clock is represented by an ostinato on pizzicato strings; then whirring higher strings, high-pitched woodwind; harsh muted brass, *crescendo*; the clock strikes eight.
A quick release: kettle drum struck ***ff***, immediately followed by a roll, *piano*, and a sustained note on bass clarinet.

Second build-up (Boris imagines the ghost of the murdered Dmitri is approaching him): much of the tension is built up by the dramatic vocal acting of the singer – supported and enhanced by the music becoming faster (agitated strings) and falling then rising in pitch above a sustained dominant pedal (kettle drum roll).

Another swift release: thump on kettle drum (resolution of dominant pedal to tonic); brass, *ff*, falling in pitch; a *crescendo* roll on kettle drum, another thump, then ending with a unison, *diminuendo*.

Page 174 Composing

Students might notate their background music in the form of a graphic score, with explanatory key.

Page 175 Linked listening – recordings on cassettes

Item	Cassette
Beethoven: fourth movement, 'Storm', from Symphony No.6 (*Pastoral*)	'Discovering Music' Book 1
Weber: The Incantation Scene in the Wolf's Glen from *Der Freischütz* ('Musical Forms' Book 3, page 14)	'History of Music', cassette 2
Wagner: final scene of *Das Rheingold* ('Musical Forms' Book 3, page 16)	'History of Music', cassette 2
Saint-Saëns: *Danse macabre*	'Enjoying Music' Book 1
Tchaikovsky: *Scène* from *Swan Lake*	'Adventures in Music' Book 2
Grieg: *In the Hall of the Mountain King* from *Peer Gynt*	'Discovering Music' Book 1
Ives: *The Housatonic at Stockbridge* from *Three Places in New England*	'Performing and Responding', CD
Britten: Fugue from *The Young Person's Guide to the Orchestra*	'Instruments of the Orchestra', (final item)

Listening Assignment K

Answers

Scène from *Swan Lake* by Tchaikovsky

The melody on which Tchaikovsky bases this music has two parts, (a) and (b):

1 The instrument playing the melody is:

a flute [ ] an oboe [✓]

a horn [ ] a clarinet [ ]

2 The sounds suggesting ripples on a lake, gleaming in the moonlight, are played on:

harp

3 The other instruments, playing a rustling accompaniment, all belong to the:

woodwind family [ ] brass family [ ] string family [✓]

4 When the melody is repeated, the first part (a) is played loudly by four horns. The second part (b) is played by:

violins

5 Two ways in which Tchaikovsky now builds up tension and excitement are:

Any two of: *crescendo* to ***ff***; *accelerando* (getting faster); use of high pitch; full orchestra involved, with heavy brass thickening the texture; rhythmic urgency (triplets); thumps and rolls on kettle drums, agitated *tremolo* strings.

(Continued on sheet 2)

6 After the music comes striding down, the opening of the melody is played *fff*. Then Tchaikovsky relaxes the tension. Describe how he does this.

> The music becomes quieter, and lower in pitch (opening of melody played ***f*** by flute, oboe and clarinet; then ***mf*** by bassoons, cellos and double basses, *diminuendo* to ***p***); the texture thins out.

7 This music is in the key of:

D major ☐ D minor ☐ B minor ☑ B major ☐

8 Describe the mood, or atmosphere, of this music:

> At first: mysterious, sad (melancholy, wistful);
> then later: menacing, dramatic, rather sinister.

CHAPTER 23 More musical devices

Students' book: pages 176–184

Summary of students' material

motive
treble (right hand), bass (left hand)
inversion
two-part contrapuntal texture
retrograde
musical palindrome
outline of minuet and trio form
retrograde inversion
canon
canon at the unison, octave, 4th, 5th
other varieties of canon (chart)

Composer	Music	Genre/form/style	Culture/country of origin
CD 3.24 Bach	Invention No.1 in C	two-part invention	Germany
(Bach)	other performances/arrangements of Invention No.1 in C	———	———
Haydn	second movement from Piano Sonata in A (Hoboken No.26; Landon No.41)	Minuet and Trio from a piano sonata; musical palindrome	Austria
CD 3.25 Haydn	third movement from Symphony No. 47 in G (orchestral arrangement of the above)	Minuet and Trio from a symphony; musical palindrome	Austria
CD 3.26 Franck	last movement of Violin Sonata in A	violin sonata; canon	Belgium

Page 177 The score opposite shows Bach's use of the motive in his Invention No.1 in C.

(O. = original version. I. = in inversion.)

The motive – either in its original version, or in inversion – appears in every bar except three: bars 6, 14 and 22.

Inventio 1
J. S. Bach

Page 177 Using *Notate*

An extension activity could be an investigation of 'Bach2ptB♭' in the *Notate* Songs directory. See the copymaster worksheet on page 129 of this Resource Book.

Answer ('Bach2ptB♭')

The motive first appears in both treble and bass at the same time in bar 9 – in inversion in the treble, original version in the bass.

Page 179 Answer

The pairs of wind instruments featured in the Trio are 2 oboes and 2 horns.

Page 180 Answers (Performing)

1 The second part imitates the first at a distance of one bar.
2 A 4th (below).

Answers (Listening)

1 The violin now leads; the piano imitates.
2 At a distance of one bar.

Page 183 Using *Notate*

1 It is possible to write a score of the palindromic rhythm canon (Composing idea No. 4) quite quickly on *Notate*, using the Copy facility. Page 130 of this Resource Book could be photocopied and handed out to students for them to follow the instructions. Or, pages 131–133 could be photocopied and handed out for immediate performance.

2 The two-part canon, Composing idea No. 5(a), can also be worked on *Notate*, making use of the Copy, Mixer, and Transpose facilities. See the copymasters on pages 134 and 135. Page 136 shows a sample printout.

Page 184 Linked listening – recordings on cassettes

Item	Cassette
Machaut: *Ma fin est mon commencement*	'Performing and Responding', CD
Anonymous: *Sumer is icumen in*	'Enjoying Early Music'
Bach: Chorale Prelude *In dulci jubilo*	'Musical Forms: Listening Scores'
Mahler: third movement (opening) of Symphony No.1	'New Assignments and Practice Scores', cassette 1 item 23
Britten: *Old Joe Has Gone Fishing* from *Peter Grimes* ('Musical Forms' Book 3, page 26)	'History of Music', cassette 2

Page 177 **Using *Notate***

Bach2ptBb

Load the song 'Bach2ptB♭' from the *Notate* Songs directory. Then use:

- the small music facility – press F7 on the keyboard;
- the full screen facility – with the mouse, click with *select* on the 'toggle size' icon, top right corner of the window.

The music is Bach's Two-part Invention No. 14 in B♭ major. He bases the piece on this six-note motive:

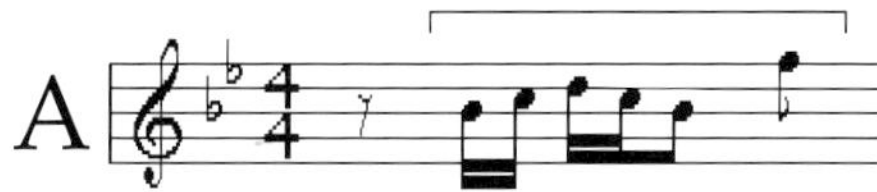

and its inversion (the motive 'turned upside down'):

In the first six bars of the piece, the motive appears six times in the treble (right hand) – sometimes in its original version (music A, above), sometimes in inversion (music B).

Then it appears alternately in the bass (left hand) and treble (right hand).

Listen to the first part of the piece. In which bar does the motive first appear in both treble and bass at the same time?

(The tempo is set at ♩ = 100. You may prefer to set a slower tempo – for example, ♩ = 84, or ♩ = 76.)

Play the whole piece, spotting other appearances of the motive – both in its original version, and in inversion.

Page 183 Using *Notate*

Palindromic Rhythm Canon

It is possible to write a score of the palindromic rhythm canon quite quickly on *Notate*, using the Copy facility.

- Open up a window, and set up three percussion tracks.
- Write the four-bar rhythm pattern (page 183) in track 1. (*Notate* will not be able to add the accents.)
- Now highlight the four-bar rhythm as a grey block – move the mouse pointer to the left of the first note, press and hold down *select* and drag the pointer to the right until you include the last note. Click with *menu* and move the pointer to the word Edit. Pass right, highlighting the word Copy in black, and click with *select*. Move the insert pointer to the beginning of bar 5 of track 1 and click with *select*. Bars 1–4 will be copied into bars 5–8.
- Highlight bars 1–8 of track 1 and copy them, in the same way, into bars 9–16. (Add more repetitions of the four-bar pattern if you wish.) Add a double bar (‖) at the end of the last bar.
- Highlight all but the last bar of track 1 as a grey block. Copy this into track 2 – beginning at bar 2.
- Highlight all but the last bar of track 2, and copy this into track 3 – beginning at bar 3.
- Add a semibreve rest (▬) to each of the three empty bars at the beginning of the piece.
- Decide whether to adjust the last half of the final bar in tracks 2 and 3 to be a minim (as track 1) so that all three parts will end up neatly and together.
- Now select three very different percussion voices, one for each track. Play back, and assess. Do the three parts of the canon stand out clearly?
- The tempo setting is ♩ = 120. Try other settings and decide which one is most musically effective.
- You could also experiment with mixing the sound levels. Press F6 on the keyboard to see the sound mixer. While the piece is playing, adjust the relative volumes of the three tracks – click with *select* on the green arrows above and below the three volume sliders. Which balance of volume settings do you think sounds most effective?
- Print out copies of the canon. Add the accents (as on page 183). Perform the canon, in a group of three musicians, each with a contrasting percussion instrument.

Palindromic Rhythm Canon

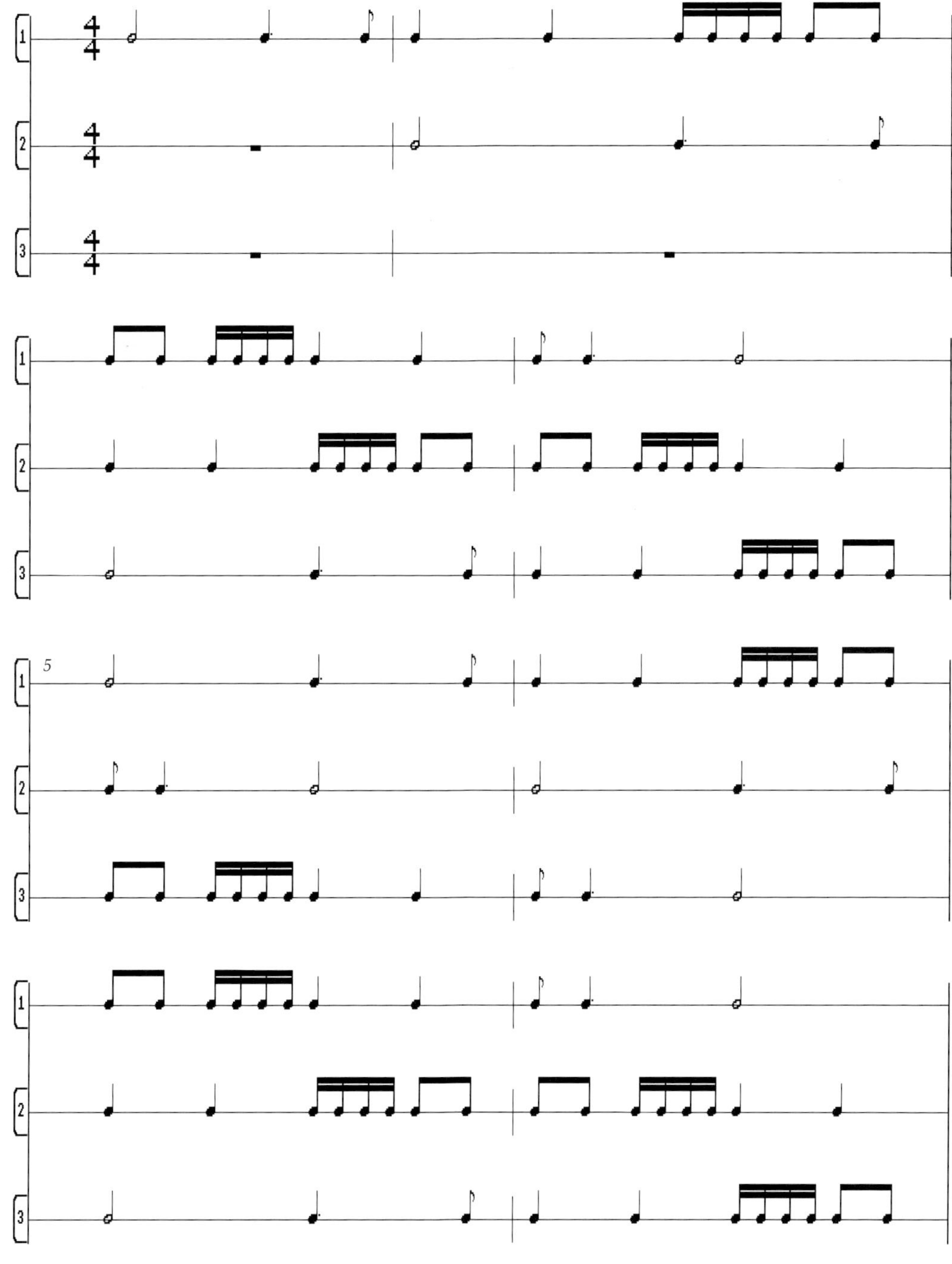

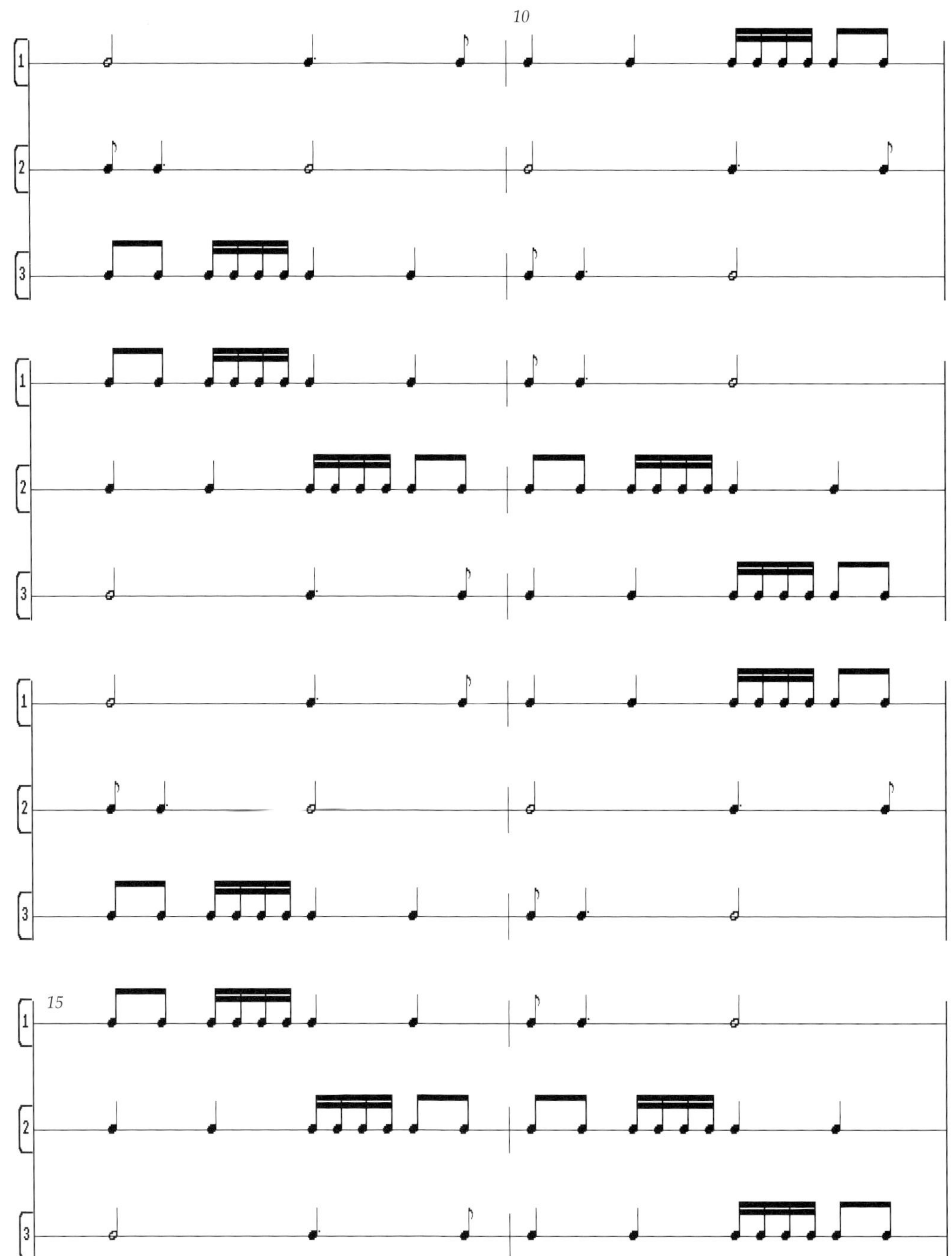
10
1
2
3
1
2
3
1
2
3
15
1
2
3

1
2
3
1
2
3
20

Page 183 Using *Notate*

Two-part Canon

The two-part canon, Composing idea No. 5(a), can be worked on *Notate*, making use of the Copy, Mixer, and Transpose facilities.

1 Open up a window. Hold down Ctrl on the keyboard and press F7. With the mouse, change the time signature to $\frac{3}{4}$. Click with *select* on OK.
Notate the tune (page 183) on track 1.
Change the tempo setting to ♩ = 110.

2 Canon at the unison
Add track 2, with a treble clef (hold down Ctrl and press F5).
Insert a semibreve rest (▬) in bar 1.
Now highlight bars 1–5 of track 1 as a grey block – move the mouse pointer to the left of the first note, press and hold down *select* and drag the pointer to the right until you include the last note of bar 5. Release *select*. Click with *menu* and move the pointer to the word Edit. Pass right, highlighting the word Copy in black, and click with *select*. Move the insert pointer to the beginning of bar 2 of track 2 and click with *select*. The music will be copied.
Play back, and assess.
Decide which notes to add to bars 7 and 8 of track 2 to make a satisfactory ending.
Play back, and assess.
Select contrasting voices for the two tracks (e.g. clarinet, vibraphone). Play back. Do the two parts in the canon stand out more clearly?

3 Canon at the octave below
Add track 3, with a bass clef (hold down Ctrl and press F5).
Copy the whole of track 2 into track 3 (*Notate* will take the pitch down *two* octaves).
Press F6 on the keyboard, and the sound mixer will appear. Turn down the volume completely on track 2 (press and hold down *select* on the bottom green arrow of track 2). Close the window.
Play back, and assess.

4 Canon at the 4th below
Add track 4, with a treble clef.
Insert a semibreve rest in bar 1.
Copy bars 1–5 of track 1 into track 4, beginning at bar 2.
Hold down Ctrl on the keyboard and press F6 to open up the Transpose dialogue box. Select track, and make it '4'. Transpose down by five semitones – move the pointer to the left-hand green arrow and click with *select* until '-5' is shown in the box. Click on OK.
Press F6 on the keyboard, and turn down the volume completely on track 3. Close the window.
Play back, and assess.

(Continued on sheet 2)

Decide which notes to add to bars 7 and 8 of track 4 to make a satisfactory ending.
Play back, and assess.
Select a suitable voice for track 4.

5 Canon at the semitone below
Add track 5, with a treble clef.
Insert a semibreve rest in bar 1. (If you can't see track 1 *and* track 5, even with the music at small size, press F8 on the keyboard and scroll the lower half of the split window until track 5 is in view. To return the split window to normal, press F8 again.)
Copy bars 1–5 of track 1 into bars 2–6 of track 5.
Hold down Ctrl on the keyboard and press F6. Select track, and make it '5'. Transpose down by one semitone. Click on OK.
Press F6 on the keyboard, and turn down the volume completely on track 4. Close the window.
For voices, try Vibraphone on track 1 and Xylophone on track 5.
Play back, and assess.
Decide which notes to add to bars 7 and 8 of track 5 to make a satisfactory ending.
Play back, and assess.

Which of the four versions of the canon do you think is most effective?
Which is least effective? Why?

(You can swiftly select any two of the five tracks to sound together by displaying the sound mixer (press F6) and clicking with *adjust* on the required track numbers at the bottom of the window. The other tracks will not be heard, regardless of the positions of the volume sliders.)

Two-part Canon

CHAPTER 24 Variations

Students' book: pages 185–189

Summary of students' material

'disguising' a well-known tune

variation form/theme and variations

ways of varying a theme (chart)

investigating variations from Tchaikovsky's Orchestral Suite No. 3

Composer	Music	Genre/form/style	Culture/country of origin
———	*God Save the Queen/America*	———	Great Britain/USA
	(1)	with changed rhythm and metre	variation
	(2)	melody decorated	variation
	(3)	in the minor key	variation
CD 3.27 Tchaikovsky	Theme from last movement of Orchestral Suite No. 3 in G	theme	Russia
CD 3.28 Tchaikovsky	Variations 1–8, from the same	variations	Russia
———	*The Green Grass*	folk-tune	England

Page 185 **Answer** (Third version of the tune)

The tune has been put into the minor key (minor mode).

Page 187 **Variation 4**

Tchaikovsky brings in the opening phrase of the plainsong melody of the *Dies irae* (from the Requiem Mass), originally setting a poem by Thomas of Celano (died *c.* 1250):

[Day of wrath; that day when the ages shall dissolve in ashes]

Other 19th- and 20th-century composers have sometimes quoted it in their compositions to bring into the listener's mind not only the symbol of death, or horrifying thoughts of the Day of Judgement, but also fear of the supernatural. Examples include:

Berlioz: *Symphonie fantastique*, final movement
Liszt: *Totentanz* (Dance of Death) and *Dante Symphony*
Saint-Saëns: *Danse macabre* (Dance of Death)
Rachmaninov: *The Isle of the Dead* and *Rhapsody on a Theme of Paganini* (Variations 7 and 24)
Respighi: *Brazilian Impressions*, second movement: *Butantan* (in this instance, ophiophobia – a horror of snakes!).

Page 189 Linked listening – recordings on cassettes

Item	Cassette
Mozart: Variations on *Ah, vous dirai-je, maman*	'Form and Design', cassette 1
Beethoven: fourth movement from Septet in E flat	'Musical Forms: Listening Scores'
Bizet: *Prélude* to *L'Arlésienne*	'Form and Design', cassette 2
Janáček: fourth movement from the *Sinfonietta*	'Enjoying Modern Music'
Britten: *The Young Person's Guide to the Orchestra* (Variations and Fugue on a Theme of Purcell)	'Instruments of the Orchestra', cassette 2, conducted by Britten (the work is recorded in separate sections throughout the cassette)
Schoenberg: Theme and Variations 1–3 from *Variations for Orchestra*	'Enjoying Modern Music'
Jelly Roll Morton: *Dead Man Blues*	'New Assignments and Practice Scores', cassette 1 item 25
Bix Beiderbecke: *At the Jazz Band Ball*	'Investigating Musical Styles', cassette 3 item 90

CHAPTER 25 Chromatic, whole-tone, and modal

Students' book: pages 192–202

Summary of students' material

semitones, tones
major scale
diatonic, chromatic
chromatic scale
notation of chromatic notes
chromatic decorations
pedal/pedal point, tonic pedal
whole-tone scale
notation of pitches
characteristics of whole-tone music
modes
'flavour' – mood and character – of a mode
Dorian, Aeolian, Phrygian, Mixolydian
flamenco

Composer	Music	Genre/form/style	Culture/country of origin
———	*The Tortilla Seller*	folk-song	Chile
Mozart	opening of the slow movement of Symphony No. 38 in D ('Prague')	chromatic; pedal	Austria
Gershwin	opening of *Rhapsody in Blue*	chromatic	USA
CD 4.1 Debussy	*Voiles* (second piano Prelude)	whole-tone	France
———	*The Unquiet Grave*	folk-song; modal	England (Dorset)
———	*The Sprig of Thyme*	folk-song; modal	England
———	*Green Bushes*	dance-song; modal	England
CD 4.2 José Luis Teruel	*Amor gitano* (Gypsy love)	flamenco; modal	Spain
CD 4.3 Cross/Haggett/Hodges	*Gemini*	rock song	England

Page 192 Background notes on the folk-song from Chile

- Most of the folk-music of Chile shows the influence of European settlers – especially Spanish; but there still remain a few independent native musical traditions which may have pre-Columbian origins.
- Instruments mainly used include: guitar, zither, harp, double-headed drums, claves, shakers, scrapers and rasps.
- The music is characterized by lively rhythms, with frequent syncopation.
- Harmonies tend to revolve around chords I, IV and V. *The Tortilla Seller* can be harmonized with just chords I and $V^{(7)}$.

Page 192 The melody of *The Tortilla Seller* with brackets showing points where steps of a semitone occur:

The Tortilla Seller

Page 193 Answers (Listening)

1. G sharp
2. There are thirteen steps of a semitone before there is a step of a whole tone.

Page 194 Answers (*Rhapsody in Blue*)

1. Gershwin's harmonies are chromatic.
2. Gershwin includes ten notes of the chromatic scale in the melody line.
3. G natural and B natural are missing from the melody line.
   G natural is included in the accompaniment in bar 2, and B natural in bar 4.

Page 195 Answers

1 Pedal, or pedal point
2 (Sample answers) Calm; mysterious; lonely/desolate; hazy and uncertain
3 Scale (1)
4 (a) All the notes of the whole-tone scale are included in the melody line in bars 1 and 2.
(b) Similarly, all the notes of the whole-tone scale are included in the left-hand chords in bar 15.
5 (A matter of opinion – though the rocking ostinato beginning at bar 23 suggests 'sails' rather then 'veils'.)

Page 197 Answers

(a) Minor 3rd between notes 1 and 3: Dorian, Aeolian, Phrygian
(b) Major 3rd between notes 1 and 3: Mixolydian
(c) All four modes have a step of a whole tone between notes 7 and 8.

The Unquiet Grave is in the Dorian mode.
The Sprig of Thyme is in the Aeolian mode.
Green Bushes is in the Mixolydian mode.

The beginning of Vaughan Williams' version of *Dives and Lazarus* is almost identical to bars 5–8 of *The Unquiet Grave*. In the third phrase of *Dives and Lazarus*, the first ten notes are identical to the beginning of *The Unquiet Grave*.

Page 198 Further background notes on *flamenco*

- Typically, *flamenco* involves dance (*baile*) and song (*cante*) accompanied by castanets, solo guitar music (*toque*), stamping and tapping dance-steps (*zapateado*), and hand-claps (*palmada*).
- Much *flamenco* is based on the Phrygian mode – whole tone between 7th and 8th degrees, semitone between 1st and 2nd degrees (a characteristic descending phrase is: A G F E).
- The accompaniment is usually played on one (or more than one) guitar, providing an introduction (*tiento*) and then acting as both solo instrument and accompaniment.
- There are three styles of accompaniment: *rasgueado* (strumming), *paseo* (lively melodic passage-work), and *falsetas* (interludes which are improvised).

Page 199 Using *Notate*

Students could load the song 'ScarFair' (which is the folk-song *Scarborough Fair*) from the *Notate* Songs directory, and identify the mode in which the melody is written (the mode being Dorian).

Page 199 **Composing idea No. 1**

On pages 144 and 145 of this Resource Book there are sample harmonizations of the three folk-tunes on pages 196 and 197 of the student's book:

(a) *The Unquiet Grave* harmonized with three chords only: A minor, D minor, and C;

(b) *The Unquiet Grave*, using six chords: A minor, D minor (7), C, B♭, F, and G minor (7);

(c) *The Sprig of Thyme* harmonized with four chords: A minor, D minor, E minor, and C;

(d) *The Sprig of Thyme*, using six chords: A minor, D minor, G, E minor (7), F, and C;

(e) *Green Bushes* harmonized with four chords: G, F, D minor, and A minor.

Chords can be added to any of the tunes using *Notate*. However:

- *The Sprig of Thyme* – the triplet in bar 17 needs to be notated either as ♪♪♩ or as ♩♪♪
- *Green Bushes* – the melody must be notated with two crotchet rests before the first note (to make a complete bar); and the final note made into a dotted minim.

An appropriate tempo needs to be selected to suit the mood and character of each melody.

Pages 201/202 **Answers** (with a suggested mark scheme for assessment)

Introduction

- Pattern (3) matches the rhythm. *(2 marks)*

Verse 1

- The step of a whole tone between notes C and D – notes 7 and 8 of the scale/mode – provides the modal flavour *(2 marks)*
- The musical device is called a pedal, or pedal point. *(2 marks)*
  The bass begins to move at 'she *dealt* my fate . . .' *(2 marks)*

Chorus 1

- Percussion/drum kit *(2 marks)*
- Pattern (1) matches the syncopated rhythm of the ostinato. *(3 marks)*

Verse 2

- The opening mood and tempo return, including rhythm pattern (3) over a pedal (pedal point) D. *(6 marks)*

Chorus 2

- Pace: swifter, more urgent *(2 marks)*
  dynamics: louder *(2 marks)*
  rhythm: more precise and emphatic, strongly syncopated (emphasizing the mood) *(2 marks)*
  timbre: percussion included, timbres brighter, harsher even (electric guitar with distortion pedal) *(3 marks)*
  texture: thicker, more complicated, 'busier' *(2 marks)*

Interlude

- (Electric) guitar *(2 marks)*
- Bass guitar *(2 marks)*

Verse 3

- Bars 2, 3, and 6 *(6 marks)*

Chorus 3

- Ten times *(3 marks)*
- (Electronic) keyboard *(2 marks)*

Coda

- The release from the tension is effected by the sustained chord, backing the new drum rhythm and spaced-out cymbal clashes as the music slows down and becomes rather quieter. *(5 marks)*

(Total: 50 marks)

Page 202 Linked listening – recordings on cassettes

Item	Cassette
Louis Armstrong: *West End Blues*	'Investigating Musical Styles', cassette 1 item 39
Debussy: *Cloches à travers les feuilles* (extract)	'Investigating Musical Styles', cassette 1 item 6
Debussy: *Reflets dans l'eau* (extract)	'Investigating Musical Styles', cassette 3 item 84
Plainchant: *Alleluia: Pascha nostrum*	'Enjoying Early Music'
Neidhart von Reuental: *Winder wie ist nu dein Kraft*	'Enjoying Early Music'
Vaughan Williams: *Fantasia on 'Greensleeves'*	'Enjoying Music' Book 1
Black Sabbath: *Paranoid*	'Investigating Musical Styles', cassette 3 item 80

The Unquiet Grave

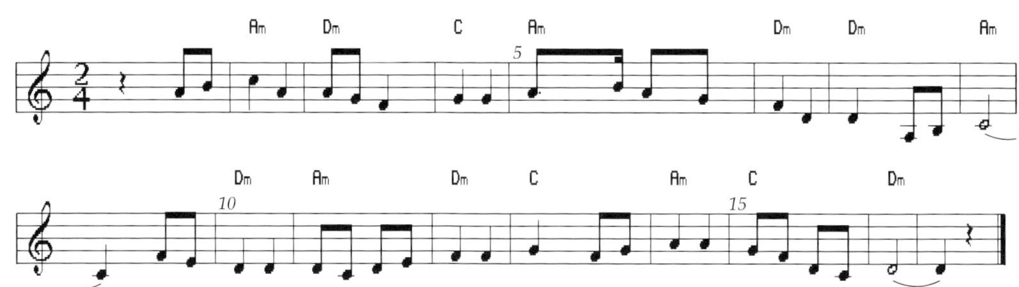

The Unquiet Grave

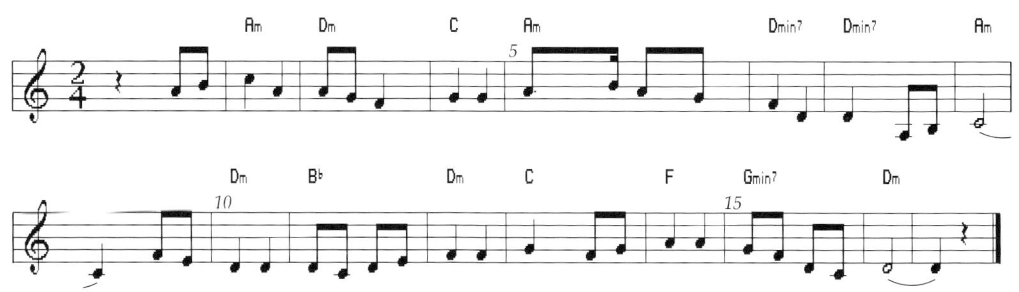

The Sprig of Thyme

The Sprig of Thyme

Green Bushes

CHAPTER 26 Timbre (3) – Exploring the voice

Students' book: pages 203–209

Summary of students' material

vocalise

Sprechgesang

varied kinds of vocal sound

treating words simply as sounds

splitting words into separate syllables, separate letters

notations of 'new' vocal sounds (chart)

Composer	Music	Genre/form/style	Culture/country of origin
CD 4.4 Rachmaninov	*Vocalise* (soprano, piano)	vocalise	Russia
CD 4.5 Berg	*Wozzeck*, Act III Scene 1	Sprechgesang	Austria
CD 4.6 Berio	*Sequenza III*	piece exploiting solo female voice	Italy
CD 4.7 George Crumb	*¿De dónde vienes, amor, mi niño?* from *Ancient Voices of Children*	song from a song-cycle	USA

Page 204 Further details of Berio's *Sequenza III*, together with the score of the first 1'20" of the piece, are given on pages 58 and 59 of 'Enjoying Modern Music'.

Page 204 **Answer** (Listening)

The various kinds of vocal sound include:
sounds at precise pitch;
sounds at approximate pitch – high, medium, low, very low;
sounds spoken at approximate pitch;
mouth clicks;
sung sounds, as short as possible;
breathy sounds, also as short as possible;
sounds with mouth closed;
with hand(s) over mouth, followed by hand(s) down from mouth;
a breathing-out sound;
sung sound – at the same time, patting mouth rapidly with hand;
and (nervous) laughter.

Page 204 **Performing/Composing**

Before tackling this, students might experiment and try out some of the vocal sounds on the chart on page 205.

Page 206 **Answer** (Third Listening)

Repetition of musical events in *¿De dónde vienes, amor, mi niño?*. Once the drumming begins, the music is structured in several short sections or musical events, A to E. In the score, these are printed in circular fashion:

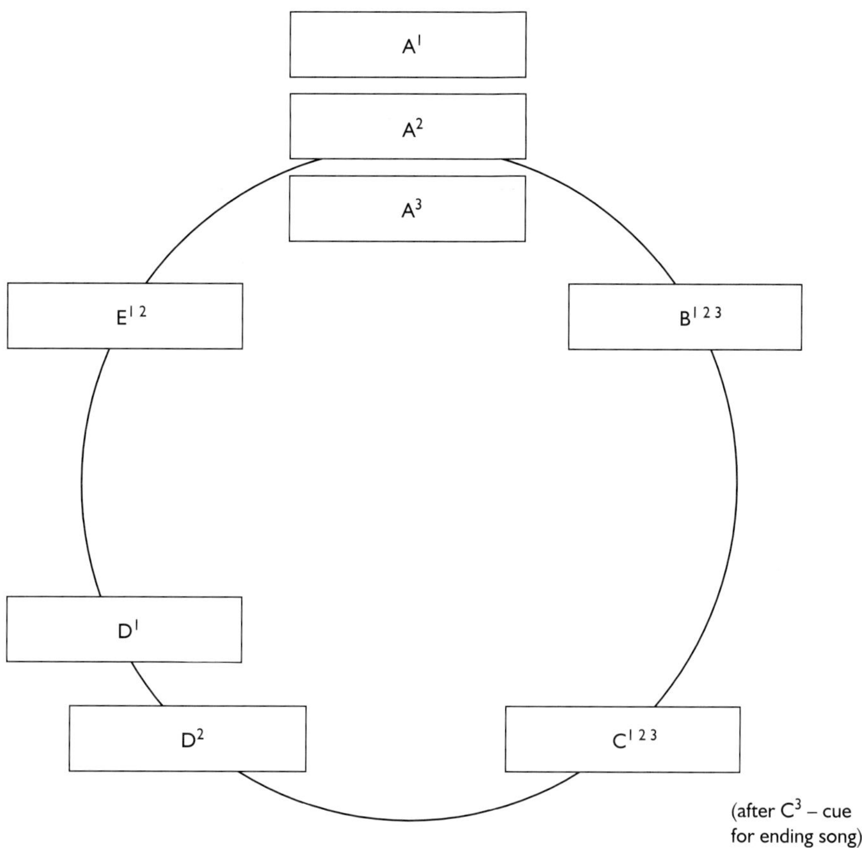

The three A sections – soprano, and boy soprano (off-stage) – use different musical material each time, as do the two D sections (D^1, boy soprano: D^2, soprano). But each of the sections B, C and E always uses the same music (repetitions):

B: oboe solo;
C: soprano, clashing glockenspiel plates, plus electric piano, harp, and mandolin (mistuned and played with metal plectrum);
E: electric piano – the pianist scrapes the strings, plays a glissando over the strings, and drums on low strings, in clusters, with bunched fingertips.

Some sections overlap slightly.

Page 206 A performance of Crumb's *Ancient Voices of Children* includes certain elements of theatre – details are given on pages 248 and 249 of the students' book.

Pages 208/209 Linked listening – recordings on cassettes

Item	Cassette
Stravinsky: *Pastorale*	'New Assignments and Practice Scores', cassette 1 item 10
Schoenberg: *Pierrot lunaire*, songs 1–5 ('Enjoying Modern Music' page 14)	'History of Music', cassette 2
Berio: second movement from *Sinfonia*	'Performing and Responding', CD
The Balinese *Kecak* dance	'Performing and Responding', CD

CHAPTER 27 Making use of physical space

Students' book: pages 210–219

Summary of students' material

musical and spatial effects
echo effects
stereo placement
spatial effects in 16th-century Venetian music
antiphony
location
Renaissance instruments

Composer	Music	Genre/form/style	Culture/country of origin
CD 4.8 Berlioz	*Tuba mirum* from the *Requiem*	Requiem	France
CD 4.9 Purcell	*In Our Deep-vaulted Cell* from *Dido and Aeneas*	echo chorus from a Baroque opera	England
CD 4.10 Mozart	first movement from *Notturno* in D (K286)	notturno (night-music)	Austria
CD 4.11 Giovanni Gabrieli	*Canzon 13*	Renaissance *canzona* (for three groups)	Italy
CD 4.12 Endsley, arranged Bob Sharples	*Singing the Blues*	arrangement of a pop song	USA/England

Pages 210/211

Answers (Berlioz)

Rhythm: varying, and with some syncopation

Melodic lines: fanfare-like motives

The drums sound various notes which form different, changing chords.

Page 211

Answers (Purcell)

1 The echoes are softer (*p*/*pp*, *f*/*mf*); there are fewer singers and instruments (no bass instruments); the echoes come from far back and to the right.

2 The main clue would be in the words/text: 'deep-vaulted cell' (cave).

Page 212

Composing

Students might notate their 'echo piece' in the form of a graphic score, with an explanatory key.

Page 216 Answers (with a suggested mark scheme for assessment)

1 Majestic, noble, dignified *(2 marks)*

2 Group 2 *(2 marks)*

3 Group 3 *(2 marks)*

4 The melodic lines move mainly by step. *(3 marks)*

5 Group 2 *(2 marks)*

6 Group 3 *(2 marks)*

7 By being dance-like in character, and in triple (instead of duple) time (the harmonic rhythm giving the impression of $\frac{3}{4} + \frac{3}{2} + \frac{3}{4}$). *(6 marks)*

8 Theme A, then B, and finally D. *(6 marks)*

9 (Any two of) C, D, E; A (bars 4–6), B (bars 14/15), F (bars 61–64). *(4 marks)*

10 By sometimes using one group alone, sometimes two, sometimes all three (full, massed sound); also by alternating between contrapuntal (polyphonic) and chordal (homophonic) textures. *(6 marks – 3 + 3)*

(Total: 35 marks)

Page 219 Linked listening

The third quarter of Stockhausen's *Gruppen* for three orchestras is recorded on 'Investigating Musical Styles', cassette 1 (item 41 A).

CHAPTER 28 Tonal and atonal

Students' book: pages 222–233

Summary of students' material

pedal/pedal point, dominant pedal
tonal, tonality
chromatic discords
factors contributing to the weakening of tonality
polytonality, conflicting tonalities
atonality
Sprechgesang
twelve-note technique/serialism
note row/basic series
original, retrograde, inversion, retrograde inversion
using the series horizontally to shape melodies, vertically to structure chords
the series merely offers basic musical material
qualities needed on the part of the composer
total serialism/integral serialism

Composer	Music	Genre/form/style	Culture/country of origin
Beethoven	opening of slow movement of Violin Sonata No. 9 in A ('Kreutzer' Sonata)	violin sonata	Germany
CD 4.13 Wagner	opening of the Prelude to *Tristan and Isolde*	operatic prelude	Germany
CD 4.14 Wagner	another extract from the same	operatic prelude	Germany
CD 4.15 Honegger	*Cortège* (Procession) from *King David*	instrumental interlude; polytonality	Switzerland
CD 4.16 Schoenberg	*Raub* (Robbery) from *Pierrot lunaire*	song-cycle; atonality; Sprechgesang	Austria
CD 4.17 ———	serial piece for solo instrument	serialism/twelve-note technique	———
CD 4.18 Berg	opening of Violin Concerto	serialism/twelve-note technique	Austria

Page 223 **Answer**

- persistant use of chromatic dissonances;
- much movement by semitone (including inner parts and bass-line);
- discords merging into further discords;
- continual, restless modulation;
- frequent *crescendi*;
- the slow, swaying $\frac{6}{8}$ metre – often with the rhythm ♩♪♩♪;
- sweeping, rising scalic passages for upper strings, increasing in urgency;
- distinctive use of large forces of woodwind, brass and strings with especially, at the climax, trumpets cutting through the texture above a roll on kettle drum.

Page 224 **Answers** (Listening)

1 The bass-line is an ostinato: 𝄆 A♭ G F G 𝄇
2 They begin *con sordini* (with mutes); then, in 6 and 7, play *senza sordini* (without mutes).
3 E minor – F minor – F major

Page 225 **Answers** (*Raub*)

1 The instruments playing the accompaniment are: flute, clarinet, violin, cello.
2 Ways in which the string instruments are played:
with mutes;
bowed *col legno* (with the wood of the bow, rather than the hair);
bowed near the fingerboard;
pizzicato;
bowed very close to the bridge;
harmonics.

Page 227 **Answers** (Listening)

In bar 14, the last note (D) of the retrograde form is omitted here since it is identical to the first note of the inversion, which follows it.

Third and fourth listenings
1 Flute
2 No
3 The last four bars are an inversion of the first four bars, and the rhythm and phrasing are identical.

Page 228 **Answers** (Listening)

1 Peaceful/serene, sad/elegiac, thoughtful/reflective
2 Bars 11–14 (G minor chord, D major chord in first inversion, A minor in second inversion, E major in first inversion)

Page 232 **Linked listening – recordings on cassettes**

Item	Cassette
Schoenberg: *Pierrot lunaire*, songs 1–5 ('Enjoying Modern Music' page 14)	'History of Music', cassette 2
Berg: *Wozzeck* – extracts from Act 1 Scene 3 and Act 3 Scene 2	'Investigating Musical Styles', cassette 3 items 86 and 87
Webern: No. 1 of *Five Movements for Strings*, Opus 5	'New Assignments and Practice Scores', cassette 2 item 6
Webern: No. 3 of *Five Pieces for Orchestra*, Opus 10	'New Assignments and Practice Scores', Score 12
Schoenberg: Theme and variations 1–3 from *Variations for Orchestra*	'Enjoying Modern Music'
Elisabeth Lutyens: opening of String Quartet No. 6	'New Assignments and Practice Scores', cassette 1 item 22
Stockhausen: *Gruppen* for three orchestras (extract)	'Investigating Musical Styles', cassette 1 item 41 A

Page 233 Berg used the note row of the *Lyric Suite* again in his song *Schliesse mir die Augen beide* (1925). In the voice part, the note row (in the original version only) is presented five times in succession.

CHAPTER 29 Chance and choice – aleatory music

Students' book: pages 234–243

Summary of students' material
creative decisions, choices
aleatory music
aleatory devices and procedures (chart)
notational symbols in aleatory scores (chart)
aleatory score for three performers
aleatory score for solo instrument and electronics

Composer	Music	Genre/form/style	Culture/country of origin
CD 4.19 ——	performance of one interpretation of the score on pages 238/239	aleatory	——
CD 4.20 ——	recording of the electronics part of the score on pages 240/241	aleatory	——

Page 235 Examples of aleatory scores can be found in:
New Harvard Dictionary of Music, page 548;
New Grove Dictionary of Music and Musicians, Volume 1, pages 239 to 241; also another (which seems to be printed upside down) in Volume 17, page 66;
also several in Reginald Smith Brindle's 'The New Music' (Oxford University Press, 1975), chapters 8 and 9.

Page 237 Teachers may care to reverse the order of Listening and Performing, so that students first perform and record their own interpretation of the aleatory score, listening afterwards to the version recorded on the cassette.

Page 243 Two extracts from *The Transistor Radio of St Narcissus* by Tim Souster (1943–1994) are recorded on 'Investigating Musical Styles', cassette 3 (items 88 and 89).

Souster studied music under Richard Rodney Bennett at Oxford, and later became composer-in-residence at King's College, Cambridge. He became very interested in the music of Stockhausen and, from 1971 to 1973, became his assistant in Cologne. Souster's compositions have often blended avant garde techniques with those of electronic music and also rock music. He was a member of the live electronic group Intermodulation, founded in 1969. After it disbanded, in 1976, he founded his own group OdB.

The Transistor Radio of St Narcissus was awarded first prize at the Bourges Festival in 1984. Souster also wrote music for films and television. His music for 'The Green Man' received the 1990 BAFTA award for Best TV Music. (Souster was also a keen cook; in 1992 he reached the semi-final of the BBC1 'Masterchef' series.)

CHAPTER 30 Mixed media, and the theatre element

Students' book: pages 244–249

Summary of students' material

mixed media/multimedia
ingredients which might be merged in a mixed media piece (chart)
selective listening
'mobile' audience – changes in perspective and balance of sounds
the theatre element/music theatre

Composer	Music	Genre/form/style	Culture/country of origin
CD 4.21 various	montage of various musics	mixed media	various
CD 4.22 Berio	*Sequenza V*	theatre element	Italy

Page 244 **Answer** (Listening)

The different types and styles of music include:

Rock
Electronic
Gamelan (Indonesian, Balinese)
Western/European Classical: piano music, 18th-century
Jazz (bop or bebop)
Western/European: Elizabethan madrigal (ballett)
Indian raga
Caribbean folk-song.

Pages 245/246 *HPSCHD* by John Cage, and *Revelation and Fall* by Peter Maxwell Davies

It was intended to include extracts on the accompanying CD from both these works. Regrettably, permission was refused. It is hoped that teachers possess, or will seek access to, the recordings:

HPSCHD – Nonesuch H-71224;

Revelation and Fall – HMV (EMI) ASD 2427 (coupled with Symphony No. 3, *Collages*, for orchestra and electronic tape, by Roberto Gerhard).

A suggested extract from *Revelation and Fall* starts at approximately 17'05" from the opening of the piece (beginning with a quiet section for solo upper strings and tom-toms), and lasts for approximately 6'55".

The piece is a setting of a prose-poem by the Austrian poet, Georg Trakl. Here is a translation of the lines heard in the suggested extract. Some words are repeated ('a blood-red phantom' is repeated a great many times).

A blood-red phantom with flaming sword burst into the house, fled with face as white as snow.

O bitter Death!

And a mysterious voice spoke from inside me: 'In the dark gloomy woods I broke my black horse's neck, for in his crimson eyes madness gleamed. The shadows of the elm trees engulfed me, the blue laughter of the spring, and the black coolness of the night, as I, a wild huntsman, chased a snow-white deer . . .'

The ensemble includes three percussionists playing a variety of conventional percussion instruments, some specially-constructed ones, and also 'found objects' such as large pebbles, knife-grinder, knife-edge on wet glass, ratchet on clock mechanism.

Instruments heard during the suggested extract include:

piccolo*, oboe, clarinet*, bass clarinet*, bassoon

horn*, trumpet* (sometimes muted), trombone

tom-toms*, railway guard's whistle, ratchet on clock mechanism, bass drum*, cymbals* (various sizes), knife-grinder, woodblock*, two whips*, two large pebbles*, tenor drum*, snare/side drum* (with snares lifted), metal sheet*, metal claves

*particularly prominent

Page 249

Linked Listening

The first ten minutes of Birtwistle's *Verses for Ensembles* are recorded on 'Investigating Musical Styles', cassette 1 (item 41 B).

Photocopy masters

(a) **Question sheets for evaluating compositions and performances**

Evaluating a composition

Evaluating an instrumental performance

Evaluating a vocal performance

(b) **Listening assignments**

The majority of these are aimed at students in the D to G grade band. The teacher may judge when times are suitable to introduce these worksheets. However, they could link to the following chapters:

	Assignment	Chapter
A	Extract from Prelude to the opera *Carmen* by Bizet*	1
B	*Swaz hie gat umbe* and *Chume, chum geselle min* from *Carmina burana* by Carl Orff	4
C	*The Fool on the Hill* by Lennon and McCartney*	5
D	Minuet in D from *Music for the Royal Fireworks* by Handel	7
E	Norwegian Dance No. 2 by Grieg	9
F	*Svevende Jord*, composed and performed by Tone Hulbaekmo*	12
G	First movement from *Venetian Games* by Lutosławski*	13
H	*The Little Train of the Caipira* by Villa-Lobos and *Pacific 231* by Honegger	15
I	English Dance No. 4 by Malcolm Arnold and *Masks* from the ballet *Romeo and Juliet* by Prokofiev	18
J	*The Devil's Dance* from *The Soldier's Tale* by Stravinsky	20
K	*Scène* from *Swan Lake* by Tchaikovsky	22

*included on the *fortissimo!* CDs

It is intended that:

- teacher and students read through (discuss) questions before listening;
- the teacher plays the music as many times as necessary;
- students use pencil rather than pen (in case of second thoughts);
- students tick the little boxes of their choice, and write in the bigger boxes.

An additional copy of each worksheet, with answers, will be found in section 2 of this Resource Book, at the end of each relevant chapter, as listed above.

Evaluating a composition

Name .... Date ....

Title ....

Composer(s) ....

1 What impact do you think the piece has on the listener? What impression does it make? Does the music hold the listener's attention?

....

....

....

....

2 Do you think there is sufficient variety/contrast in the music (for example: of dynamics, timbre, pitch, melody, rhythm, texture)?

....

....

....

3 Which musical elements come across most strongly or effectively? Are these musical elements effectively explored, and controlled?

....

....

....

4 Is the musical style maintained right through the piece?

....

....

....

5 Does the piece have a satisfying overall *shape* (form, design, structure, balance and organization of ideas)? Is there a sense of 'wholeness', of completeness?

....

....

....

6 Is there a climax (perhaps more than one)? If so, does the music build up effectively?

....

....

....

7 Are the musical ideas original, interesting, imaginative? Are they explored, extended, developed, in effective ways?

....

....

....

....

8 Do you think that the right *medium* – instrument(s)/voice(s)/sound-source(s) – was chosen for this music? Is the chosen medium used effectively, and with understanding?

....

....

....

....

9 Does the mood and character of the music match the title and/or words of the piece?

....

....

....

10 If the music is notated, in any way, is the notation appropriate, and as clear and accurate as possible? Are clear performance directions given?

....

....

....

11 Is there anything you would change about the piece?

....

....

....

....

Evaluating an instrumental performance

Name .... Date ....

Title ....

Composer(s) ....

Performer(s) ....

1 Were you satisfied that, throughout the performance, there was accuracy of notes/pitch?

....

....

....

2 Was there accuracy of rhythm?

....

....

....

3 Did the performance make effective use of dynamics?

....

....

....

4 Was the tempo (speed) appropriate for the music?

....

....

....

5 Did you feel that the tempo (whether steady, or changing) was always under control?

....

....

....

6 Was the quality of tone (perhaps also, variations of tone) suitable to the music?

....

....

....

7 Did the performance show an understanding of the character and style of the music?

....

....

....

8 Did it show an awareness of the overall shape (form, design, structure) of the piece?

....

....

....

9 Was the interpretation of the music faithful to the composer's intentions (for example, in obeying directions of tempo, dynamics, phrasing, other expression markings)?

....

....

....

....

10 Did you feel that there was a sense of commitment, of involvement with the music, throughout the performance?

....

....

....

....

11 Was the music effectively presented and communicated to the listener?

....

....

....

....

Evaluating a vocal performance

Name .... Date ....

Title ....

Composer(s) ....

Performer(s) ....

1 Were you satisfied that, throughout the performance, there was accuracy of notes/pitch?

....

....

....

2 Was there accuracy of rhythm?

....

....

....

3 Did the performance make effective use of dynamics?

....

....

....

4 Was the tempo (speed) appropriate for the music?

....

....

....

5 Did you feel that the tempo (whether steady, or changing) was always under control?

....

....

6 Was the quality of tone (perhaps also, variations of tone) suitable to the music?

....

....

....

7 Did the performance show an understanding of the character and style of the music?

....

....

....

8 Did it show an awareness of the overall shape (form, design, structure) of the piece?

....

....

....

9 Was the interpretation of the music faithful to the composer's intentions (for example, in obeying directions of tempo, dynamics, phrasing, other expression markings)?

....

....

....

10 Did you feel that there was a sense of commitment, of involvement with the music, throughout the performance?

....

....

11 Was the music effectively presented and communicated to the listener?

....

....

....

12 Was there good breath control throughout the performance?

....

....

13 Were you satisfied that the diction (the singing of vowels, consonants) was sufficiently clear?

....

....

14 Do you think the performance was successful in expressively bringing out the mood and meaning of the words?

....

....

....

Listening Assignment A

Extract from Prelude to the opera *Carmen* by Bizet

1 The instruments you hear first are:

woodwind ☐ brass ☐ percussion ☐

2 Then the tune is played by:

violins ☐ trumpets ☐ clarinets ☐

3 The music is in the style of:

a waltz ☐ a march ☐ a jig ☐

4 The tune is played again – with the full orchestra joining in. The tune is now played:

(a) higher than before ☐ lower than before ☐

and (b) more quietly ☐ more loudly ☐

5 You now hear a different tune.
Two percussion instruments which add excitement and brilliance to the music are:

(a)

(b)

6 At the end of the piece, the music:

slows down ☐ gets quicker ☐ keeps the same speed ☐

7 The mood of this music is:

dreamy ☐ solemn ☐ joyful ☐ mysterious ☐

8 What do you like, or dislike, about this music?

Listening Assignment B

Swaz hie gat umbe and *Chume, chum geselle min* from *Carmina burana* by Carl Orff

These two songs are for two groups of voices – women's voices, and men's voices. The accompaniment is for orchestra.

Carl Orff makes effective use of repetition and contrast. The music of the first half of Song 2 is repeated for the second half. After Song 2, there is a repeat of Song 1. There are strong musical contrasts between the two songs.

Song 1

At first, the two groups of voices swiftly alternate.

(a) The first group of voices you hear are:

women's voices ☐ men's voices ☐

(b) The second group of voices:

repeats the music of the first group ☐ sings completely different music ☐

(c) Two percussion instruments which add colour and excitement to the last part of Song 1 are:

(1)

(2)

Song 2

(d) The first voices you hear are:

women's voices ☐ men's voices ☐

(e) They are singing:

in unison ☐ in two parts ☐

(f) Next to sing are:

women only ☐ men only ☐ men and women together ☐

(g) They are singing:

in unison ☐ in harmony ☐

(Questions continued on sheet 2)

(h) Name the instrument which plays a solo when the singing stops.

(i) The music of Song 2 is:

faster than Song 1 ☐ slower than Song 1 ☐

(j) The dynamic level is:

quieter than Song 1 ☐ louder than Song 1 ☐

(k) The music of Song 2 has:

2 beats to a bar ☐ 3 beats to a bar ☐ 5 beats to a bar ☐

Repeat of Song 1

(l) The tempo of Song 1 is:

moderate ☐ fairly fast ☐ very fast ☐

(m) Just after the women and men start to sing *together*, the music:

slows down for a moment ☐ gets very much faster ☐

(n) A dynamic marking for this song would be:

p ☐ ***mp*** ☐ ***mf*** ☐ ***ff*** ☐

(o) A performance of these two songs creates this musical form:

A Song 1	**B** Song 2 (contrast)	**A** Song 1 (repeated)

The name given to this musical form is:

(p) Which of the two songs do you like best? Why?

Listening Assignment C

The Fool on the Hill by Lennon and McCartney

(CD item 1.13 – consisting of two verses of the song)

1 The melody is first played on:

piccolo ☐ clarinet ☐

alto saxophone ☐ horn ☐

2 The number of beats to a bar is:

two ☐ three ☐ five ☐

3 Listen for the music to slip from major into minor. What particular sound emphasizes the effect?

4 When the music slips back into the major, you hear:

a rising major scale ☐ steadily repeated major chords ☐

5 At the beginning of verse 2, the melody is played by:

6 A suitable dynamic marking for the music would be:

7 In the second (minor key) part of each verse, stabbing chords are played:

on the beat ☐ off the beat ☐

8 The melody of this song moves:

mainly by step ☐ mainly by wide leap ☐

9 A suitable tempo marking for the music would be:

Adagio ☐ Moderato ☐ Presto ☐

Listening Assignment D

Minuet in D from *Music for the Royal Fireworks* by Handel

1 In the box after the key signature, write the correct time signature.

2 Add the missing notes in the empty bars 6 and 7.

3 Explain the meaning of :‖ at the end of bar 8 and the end of bar 16.

> end of bar 8:
>
> end of bar 16:

4 The key of this music is D major. Bars 1 to 8 use only two chords:

chord I (tonic chord) = chord of ☐

chord V (dominant chord) = chord of ☐

In the boxes below bars 1 to 8, fill in the missing symbols. Four of them have already been done for you.

5 The music of bars 9 and 10 is repeated in bars 11 and 12 at a lower pitch. Write the name for this musical device in the box below bar 11.

6 A suitable dynamic marking for this Minuet would be:

☐

Listening Assignment E

Norwegian Dance No. 2 by Grieg

Grieg structures this dance in three sections of music.

First section

1 The tune is played by an oboe. Which of these shapes matches the opening notes of the tune?

(a) ☐ (b) ☐ (c) ☐

2 How are the string instruments being played to produce this kind of sound?

☐

3 The tune is immediately repeated. How are the violins played now?

☐

Second section

4 The music of this section is:

(a) louder ☐ quieter ☐ and (b) slower ☐ faster ☐

5 The texture of the music is:

richer, denser than before ☐ clearer, thinner than before ☐

6 How does this second section end?

☐

Third section

7 Does this section use the same tune as the first section, or does it use a completely new tune?

☐

8 The music of this Norwegian Dance is:

in $\frac{2}{4}$ time ☐ in $\frac{3}{4}$ time ☐

9 The music is structured in:

binary form ☐ ternary form ☐ rondo form ☐

Listening Assignment F

Svevende Jord (Floating Earth), composed and performed by Tone Hulbaekmo

This music is structured in two contrasting sections.

First section

1 Arrange these in the order you hear them:

wooden flute　　girl's voice　　synthesizer

Write your answers in these boxes:

(a)	(b)	(c)

2 The speed of this music is:

slow ☐　　fast ☐　　fairly fast ☐

3 The music of this section is:

always loud ☐　　always quiet ☐

sometimes loud, sometimes quieter ☐

Second section

4 The music changes. Which two of these instruments do you hear?

violin ☐　　wooden flute ☐　　tambourine ☐　　bass guitar ☐

5 When the singing begins, the synthesizer plays:

high-pitched notes ☐　　low-pitched notes ☐

6 Compared with the music of the first section, this music is:

more rhythmic ☐　　less rhythmic ☐

7 Just before the recording fades, the music:

slows down ☐　　gets faster ☐

8 Which section of the piece do you like best? Why?

Listening Assignment G

First movement from *Venetian Games* by Lutosławski (Poland; 1913–1994)

Investigate the chart on sheet 2, which shows how this piece is built up. There are eight sections of music, each of different duration (section 6 is only two seconds long).

You will know when each section begins because, each time, there is a loud, explosive sound on percussion. The piece ends with four bars for percussion – the instruments dropping out one by one.

1 As you listen to the music:

(a) for each section, draw a wavy line in the top part of any box where instruments are playing (sections 1, 5 and 6 are already completed for you).

(b) under each wavy line you draw, write a dynamic marking – write:

f if the music is mainly loud;

p if the music is mainly quiet;

mf if the music is moderately loud.

2 When you have completed your chart, listen to the music again and answer these questions.

(a) Which section of the piece has the heaviest, most dense, most complicated texture?

Section

(b) Give the number of a section which has a light, thin, clear texture.

Section

(c) Each section begins with a loud sound played on four percussion instruments. Name one of them.

(d) Which three of the following do you think are most important in creating the effect of the whole piece?

melody ☐ timbre ☐ texture ☐

dynamics ☐ rhythm ☐

(Continued on sheet 2)

Listening Assignment G

First movement from *Venetian Games* by Lutosławski (Poland; 1913–1994)

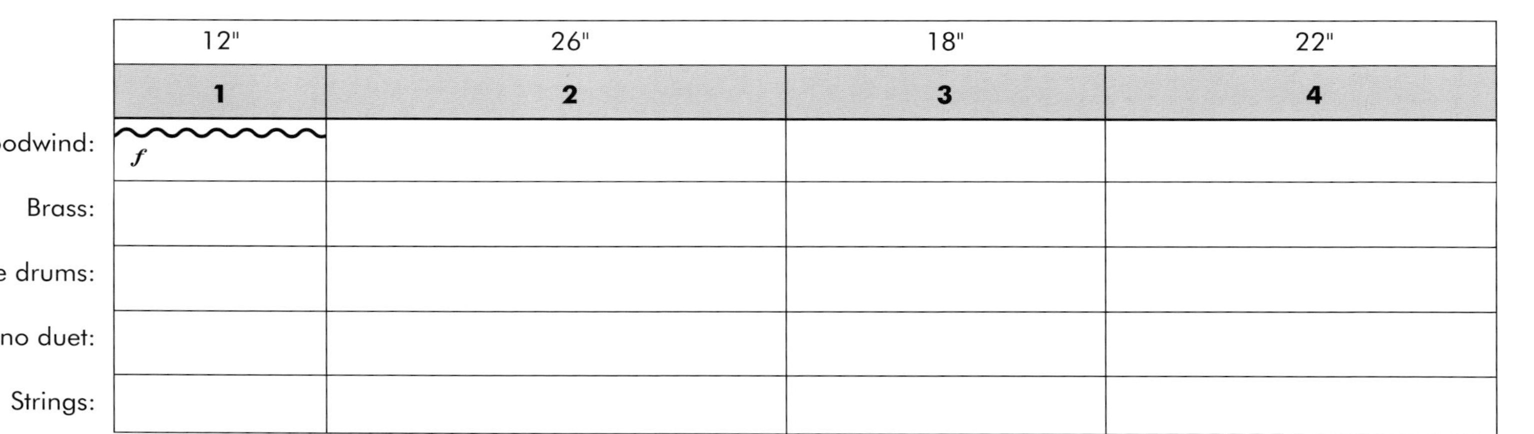

	12"	26"	18"	22"
	1	**2**	**3**	**4**
Woodwind:	~~~ *f*			
Brass:				
Kettle drums:				
Piano duet:				
Strings:				

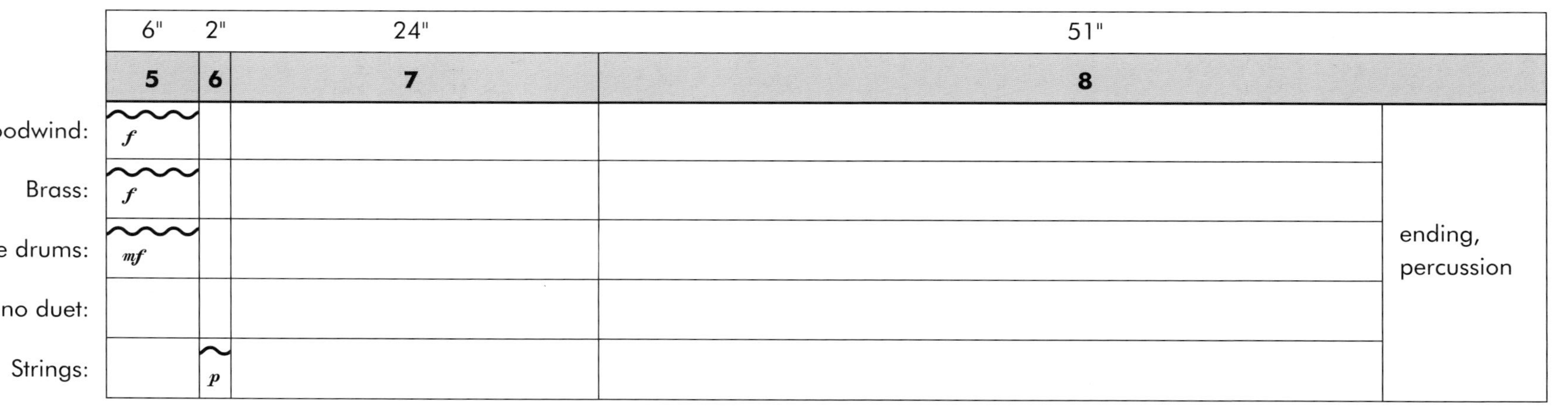

	6"	2"	24"	51"	
	5	**6**	**7**	**8**	
Woodwind:	~~~ *f*				ending, percussion
Brass:	~~~ *f*				
Kettle drums:	~~~ *mf*				
Piano duet:					
Strings:		~ *p*			

Listening Assignment H

Listen to two pieces of programme music. Each paints a musical picture of the journey of a certain type of train:

A: *The Little Train of the Caipira* by Villa-Lobos

B: *Pacific 231* by Honegger

(A *caipira* is a Brazilian countryman. A locomotive of the 'Pacific' type would be used for heavy trains and high speed.)

In each of the following pairs of items, match one item to each piece. In the boxes, write:

A for the items which match *The Little Train of the Caipira*,

B for the items which match *Pacific 231*.

1 Low-pitched instruments (such as double basses) tell you when this train starts to move. ☐

Percussion instruments (such as various rattles and scrapers) tell you this train is starting to move. ☐

2  ☐  ☐

3  ☐  ☐

4  ☐  ☐

(Questions continued on sheet 2)

5 Rhythm of each main tune:

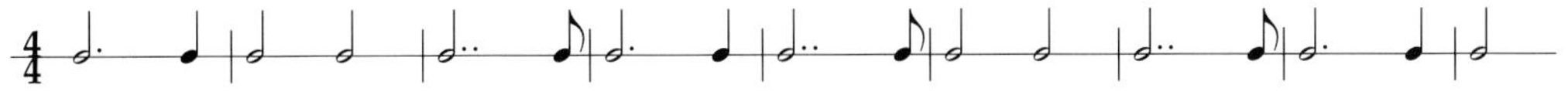

☐

☐

6 This train travels at more or less the same speed throughout its journey. ☐

During its journey, this train almost stops – but then picks up speed again. ☐

7 In this piece, the music ends as soon as the train has stopped. ☐

In this piece, the music continues for a while after the train has stopped. ☐

Which of these two pieces of programme music do you think is the most effective? In what ways?

Listening Assignment I

Listen to two contrasted dances:

A: English Dance No. 4 by Malcolm Arnold

B: *Masks* from the ballet *Romeo and Juliet* by Prokofiev

In each of the eight musical categories below, match the descriptions to the dances. In the boxes, write:

A if the description matches English Dance No. 4, or

B if the description matches *Masks*.

(Use pencil – in case you have second thoughts!)

1	**Tempo:**	moderate speed	☐	fairly fast	☐
2	**Melody:**	medium in range, moving by step and narrow leap	☐	wide in range, and including wide leaps	☐
3	**Metre:**	3 beats to a bar	☐	4 beats to a bar	☐
4	**Rhythm:**	regular, steady	☐	much use of syncopation	☐
5	**Texture:**	mainly heavy, rich, dense	☐	mainly light, clear, open	☐
6	**Harmonies:**	mainly concords	☐	spicy discords at times	☐
7	**Dynamics:**	very loud (*ff*) almost throughout	☐	varying over a wide range (*pp* to *ff*)	☐
8	**Character:**	forceful, energetic, heavy-footed	☐	carefree, jaunty, bouncy	☐

Which of these two dances do you like best? Why?

Listening Assignment J

The Devil's Dance from *The Soldier's Tale* by Stravinsky

A In this piece, you will hear the sounds of ten instruments. Look at this chart:

....	....	**Strings**	....
....	....	....	3 snare drums, with snares lifted
bassoon	trombone	....	....

The names of some of the instruments are already filled in. And the name of one of the four sections of the orchestra.

Listen to *The Devil's Dance*, and fill in the missing words.

B Listen again to *The Devil's Dance*. For each of these five categories, tick the description which you think best matches the music.

(1) **Melodies:** long and flowing ☐ short and spiky ☐

(2) **Dynamics:** mainly quiet ☐ mainly loud ☐

(3) **Tempo:** quite fast ☐ fairly slow ☐

(4) **Rhythms:** energetic, syncopated ☐ smooth, relaxed ☐

(5) **Harmonies:** mainly concords ☐ mainly discords ☐

C Look at the group of instruments on the right. Name the instrument in the group which does *not* take part in *The Devil's Dance*.

☐

Name the instruments which take part in *The Devil's Dance* which are *missing* from the group.

☐

Listening Assignment K

Scène from *Swan Lake* by Tchaikovsky

The melody on which Tchaikovsky bases this music has two parts, (a) and (b):

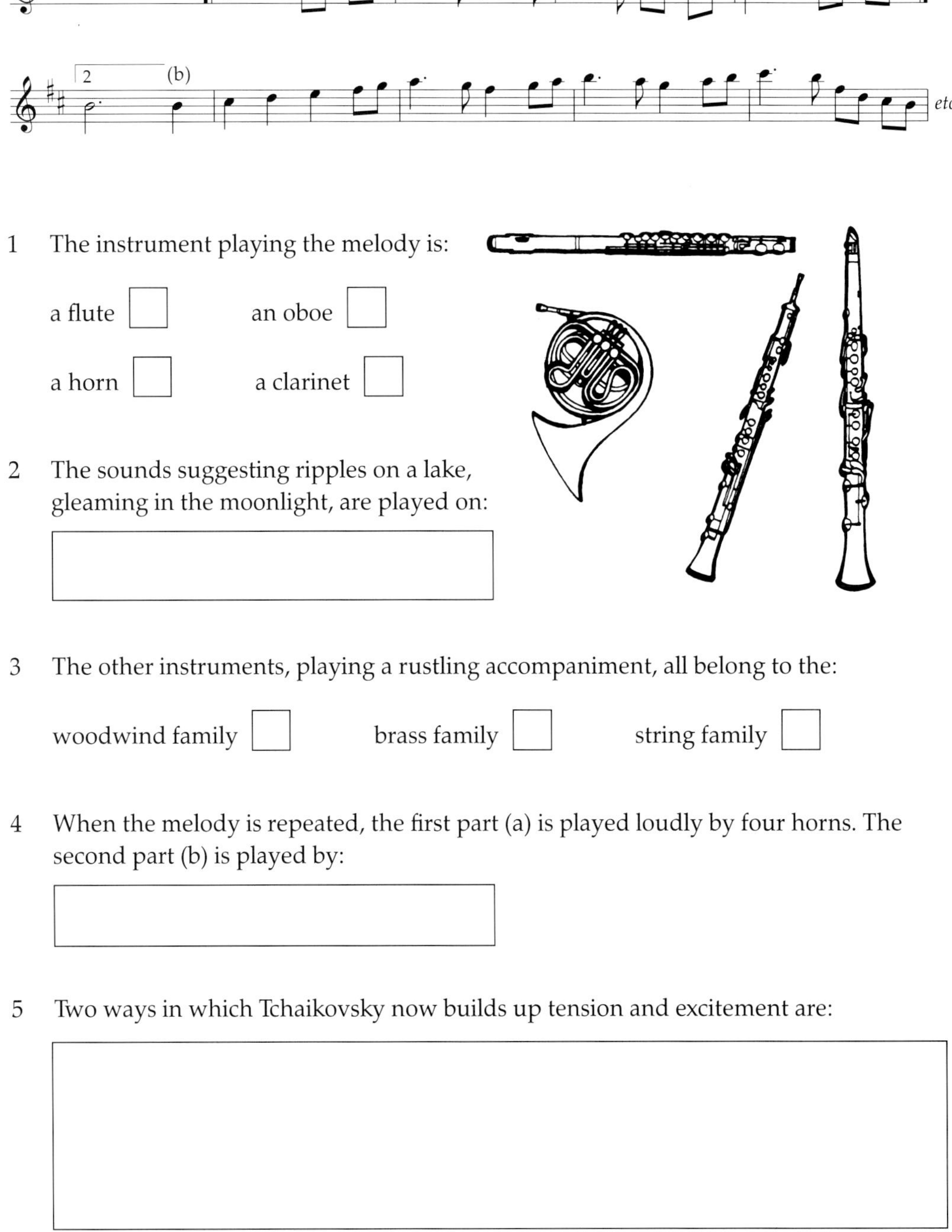

1 The instrument playing the melody is:

a flute ☐ an oboe ☐

a horn ☐ a clarinet ☐

2 The sounds suggesting ripples on a lake, gleaming in the moonlight, are played on:

3 The other instruments, playing a rustling accompaniment, all belong to the:

woodwind family ☐ brass family ☐ string family ☐

4 When the melody is repeated, the first part (a) is played loudly by four horns. The second part (b) is played by:

5 Two ways in which Tchaikovsky now builds up tension and excitement are:

(Questions continued on sheet 2)

6 After the music comes striding down, the opening of the melody is played *fff*. Then Tchaikovsky relaxes the tension. Describe how he does this.

7 This music is in the key of:

D major ☐ D minor ☐ B minor ☐ B major ☐

8 Describe the mood, or atmosphere, of this music:

Details of items included on the double-page coloured spreads in the students' book

Spread A, pages 32/33

- Pine needles and cones of the *Cedrus atlantica* (Atlas cedar)
- Stalactites and stalagmites, Nerja caves, Andalusia, southern Spain
- The Rolling Stones
- Cut gem stones in varying colours, shapes, textures
- Fireworks display
- String of black bryony berries, ripening from green, through yellow and orange, to bright scarlet

Spread B, pages 54/55

- A spectacular pattern in process of being created by 126 skydivers over Belgium, May 1987
- Medieval shawm-players accompanying a round-dance in a castle garden
- Light and shade: sunlit reeds reflected in water against a shadowy background
- Scene from a Balinese dramatic dance, accompanied by gamelan
- Liz Young, showjumper
- Varying speeds: steady, constant movement of cable car contrasting with huge rollercoaster – slowly climbing, then rushing downwards

Spread C, pages 76/77

- Rainbow colours caused by light reflecting on the surface of a soap bubble
- The symmetrical, tripartite West front of Wells Cathedral, Somerset (1230–1239)
- Crystals of purple fluorite (calcium fluoride)
- Jazz musicians performing in Maison Bourbon, New Orleans – the 'cradle of jazz' in the deep south of the USA
- Beginning of a graphic score
- Chinese ideogram for the word 'music'
- Red admiral butterfly (*Vanessa atalanta*)

Spread D, pages 100/101

- Mechanical works of the clock of Wells Cathedral
- Neuschwanstein Castle, Bavaria, Germany
- 'Japanese Print' (print stamping and screen printing on coloured tissue paper) by a Year 6 art group
- 'He Wishes for the Cloths of Heaven' from William Butler Yeats's collection of poems entitled 'The Wind Among the Reeds'(1899)
- Graphics representing sequence, and imitation
- Fountain pieces at the Pompidou Centre, Paris
- Morning mist over the Grand Canyon (gorge of the Colorado River), Arizona, USA

Spread E, pages 122/123

- Moonlight on rocks and calm sea
- Description by Charles Ives after a Sunday morning walk with his wife at Stockbridge, Massachusetts, USA, June 1908
- 'Shell Bay', a collage including sea shells, seaweed, handmade paper, and embroidery, by a Year 11 art and design student
- Violent waves crashing against rocky cliffs, Oregon, on the Pacific coast of the USA
- Reassembled skeleton (in the Natural History Museum, London) of a *tuojiangosaurus* – a dinosaur which lived in China 150 million years ago
- Spray of blackthorn in flower, with black hairstreak butterfly (*strymonidia pruni*)

Spread F, pages 144/145

- Magnified snowflakes in computer-enhanced colours
- Magnified jellyfish/plankton
- Varied weaving techniques, using dyed natural materials (sisal, wool, fleece, string, cotton, raffia), to suggest woven equivalents of shrubs, plants, buds, flowers, blossoms; by a Year 11 art and design student
- The Chinese and Japanese ideograms for the word 'sounds'
- Trees, in varicoloured autumn foliage, reflected in the calm waters of a lake

Spread G, pages 170/171

- Duo of break dancers
- Beginning of a score featuring note-clusters
- Rock group: The Police
- Ninga tribal drummers and acrobatic dancer, Burundi, east central Africa (north west of Tanzania)
- Opening scene of Shakespeare's 'Macbeth'
- Classical Indian dancer in typical pose of the *bharata-nāṭyam* dance style, which is the purest and most ancient of all Indian dance styles
- Mexican street musicians

Spread H, pages 190/191

- A Year 3 pupil's study after Edvard Munch's painting,'The Scream'(shown on page 65 of 'History of Music' in the Cambridge Assignments in Music series)
- Fountains, reflected in water, at Breda, North Brabant, Netherlands
- Circles of ripples produced by raindrops on a lake, Denali National Park, Alaska
- Light trails from traffic at night, down-town Toronto, Ontario, Canada
- The Forth Bridge, Scotland – a cantilever railway bridge spanning the River Forth from Lothian to Fife
- Four machine-embroidered panels, based on microscope studies of plant cells, by a Year 11 art and design student
- Coloured graphics, implying inversion, retrograde, and retrograde inversion
- One of a series of 'snarling heads' – self-portraits as sketches for a painting to be entitled 'Pandora's Box' – by a Year 11 art and design student

Spread I, pages 220/221

- Sketch-plan of the layout of a piece making use of physical space – involving 'live' musicians in conjunction with pre-recorded sounds on four-track tape
- American songwriter and performer, Bob Dylan (real name, Robert Allen Zimmerman)
- Opening lines of *Canción de jinete* (Song of the rider) by the Spanish poet, Federico García Lorca
- The double helix structure of DNA (deoxyribonucleic acid) which, within living cells, carries the genetic code for the inheritance of characteristics
- Cathy Berberian performing *Recital I*, a music-theatre piece involving many kinds of vocal sounds, styles and gestures, written for her in 1971 by Luciano Berio
- Stages in organic growth of a daffodil, evolving from bud to full-blown flower – time lapse multiple exposure over the time-span of one week

Spread J, pages 250/251

- The printed circuit board of a video tape recorder
- 'Pomegranate', a mobile structured from sheet aluminium, steel wire and rods, by the American, Alexander Calder (inventor of the mobile)
- Two dice and a coin – suggesting chance operations in composing a piece of music
- Beginning of an aleatory composition for six instrumentalists and electronic sounds on pre-recorded tape
- A computer-enhanced colour photograph of a total eclipse of the sun, 26 February 1979